# OHIO'S
## BLACK HAND
# SYNDICATE

# OHIO'S BLACK HAND SYNDICATE

## The Birth of Organized Crime in America

David Meyers and Elise Meyers Walker

THE
History
PRESS

Published by The History Press
Charleston, SC
www.historypress.com

Copyright © 2018 by David Meyers
All rights reserved

First published 2018

Manufactured in the United States

ISBN 9781467139762

Library of Congress Control Number: 2017963232

*In memory of my parents, Virgil and Marie Meyers.*
*I stand on their shoulders.*

# CONTENTS

# CONTENTS

# ACKNOWLEDGEMENTS

T hanks to Evelyn Keener Walker for her suggestions, Tara Narcross for her advice, Randy McNutt for his encouragement and John Rodrigue for his support. Also our appreciation goes to the Library of Congress, the New York Public Library and the Columbus Metropolitan Library for the use of images from their collections.

# INTRODUCTION

*They tackled the wrong fish.*[1]
—*John Amicon*

t took awhile for crime to get organized in the United States. Despite the existence of criminal bands at least as far back as colonial days, law enforcement generally was reluctant to admit that organized crime had reached America's shores even as the twentieth century was dawning.[2] But it had, if only in a primitive form. It was brought over by "foreigners" (i.e., our ancestors) as surely as they had their languages, customs, religions, foods and diseases.

Most historians trace "true" organized crime back to Prohibition, bootleggers and the rise of the Capone mob in Chicago. Certainly, Al Capone, building on the foundation laid by Johnny Torrio by way of "Big Jim" Colosimo, constructed a criminal syndicate unlike any before it. However, it may actually have had a much humbler birth, more than a decade earlier, in the back room of a fruit store in Marion, Ohio. And the seed from which it sprouted was the Black Hand.

Although the term would not come into use until about 1898, the Black Hand, or La Mano Nera, first appeared in the United States in the 1870s and, for all intents and purposes, passed out of existence in the 1920s. A technique for extorting money through threats of violence, it was believed by many to have developed into an organized criminal conspiracy—a so-called Black Hand society—first in Italy and then in North America.

By 1878, a band of Sicilian immigrants calling themselves La Maffia was known to have been running an extortion racket in San Francisco. The *San Francisco Examiner* described the members as "a neat little tea party of Sicilian brigands" who endeavored to extort "money from their countrymen by a system of blackmail, which includes attacks on character and threats to kill."[3] This would soon come to epitomize Black Hand crime.

Early on, the terms *Mafia* and *Black Hand* were used interchangeably by law enforcement and the newspapers to describe any crimes committed by Italians. But in 1908, Gaetano D'Amato, former president of the United Italian Societies, argued that the existence of a Black Hand society in Italy was a myth. He claimed it had actually originated in Spain, where it referred to well-intentioned missionaries who had "hoped to redress the balance between rich and poor; but it soon drew down to it many desperadoes."[4]

D'Amato pointed out that both good and bad Italians had been allowed into the United States due to lax immigration laws. They included thousands of ex-convicts from Naples, Sicily and Calabria, who supported themselves by robbery and extortion. Although such criminals represented less than 3 or 4 percent of the nation's Italian population and were not organized to any significant extent, it was these individuals who "the sensational press" had branded the Black Hand. "Almost every dark-skinned European not speaking English, who does not wear the Turkish fez, is put down on the police records as an Italian, and thus the Italian is condemned for much of the crime committed here by persons of other nationalities."[5]

Even the term *Black Hand*, D'Amato claimed, was first invoked in the United States about ten years earlier by an Italian desperado who was inspired by the exploits of the Spanish. He maintained it had not been used in Italy until after it was popularized in America. Once it became associated with certain types of crimes, the newspapers ran with it, making the assumption that all such crimes were the work of one group—the elusive Black Hand Society. This was like believing all pickpockets, panhandlers or pool hustlers were in cahoots.

Alessandro Mastro-Valerio, publisher of an Italian-language newspaper in Chicago, went so far as to charge that Carlo Barsotti, editor of a rival paper in New York, had invented the term *Black Hand* in an effort to avoid using the word *Mafia* with its Old World associations. However, many historians were of the opinion that the earliest Black Hand activities began in Sicily as early as the 1750s and then spread throughout the rest of the kingdom of Naples.

Even as Italian-language newspapers were denying its existence, the Mafia was being blamed for all manner of crimes committed by and against

Italians in the United States. And there can be no denying that criminal bands were active in American cities that had colonies or settlements of immigrants from southern Italy. As immigrants from the southern regions of Italy began arriving in the 1880s, the lawbreakers among them continued their shakedown of their compatriots. By 1900, there was evidence of such blackmail efforts in the Italian American communities of many major cities, particularly New York, New Orleans and Chicago. Although the more successful immigrants were their primary targets, it was estimated that at one point nearly 90 percent of all Italians in New York had been threatened by the Black Hand.

The Black Hand brand had a certain cachet that caught the imagination of criminals and would-be criminals who freely flaunted it to suggest that they were soldiers in a larger army. If everyone who called themselves the Black Hand were part of the same villainous group, then it would have been an enormous enterprise, indeed. But they weren't. From New York to New Orleans, the Black Hand was the boogeyman, attributed with every shocking and unsolved crime.

In truth, most so-called Black Handers did not exhibit a very sophisticated or wide-ranging network. Certainly, they had nothing to match the Unione Siciliana. In the early 1880s, the Unione Siciliana was formed in New York City as a fraternal and benevolent association. It helped Sicilian immigrants by selling insurance, assisting with housing, providing English language instruction, settling legal disputes and, on occasion, endeavoring to negotiate peaceful settlements in Black Hand affairs. A Chicago branch was chartered a decade later, with membership of over half a million.

In time, however, local criminal gangs and politicians began to vie for control of the Unione Siciliana, much as they did labor unions in the 1920s and 1930s. Such outwardly respectable organizations would come to provide cover for all manner of nefarious endeavors, up to and including murder (although a few historians still deny the Unione Siciliana was ever corrupted). Giovanni Schiavo, a pioneer in Italian American studies and a proud Sicilian, dedicated himself to refuting "the drivel that has been written regarding the Black Hand and the Unione Siciliana."[6] He was adamant that there was never an American Mafia.[7]

In this work, we have set out to tell the largely forgotten story of how a bunch of so-called banana peddlers put together a multi-state extortion ring and, in doing so, became the first group in the country convicted of organized crime. Certainly, D'Amato or Schiavo would have been disappointed, but not surprised, to learn that this abominable enterprise was the work of Italian immigrants. However, they could take pride in the fact that it was broken up through the efforts of their fellow countrymen—a handful of brave Italian men who were willing to risk their lives to stand up to a pack of domestic terrorists—men such as Frank Dimaio, Victor Churches and John Amicon.

A century after the heyday of the Black Hand, the United States continues to struggle with the challenge of immigration. Most would agree that the immigration system in the United States is in shambles and rewards neither the most destitute nor the most deserving. But that should not overshadow the fact that our country needs immigrants if it is to survive and prosper. With the birth rate declining to record lows, we must have immigrants to replace the graying population. We require younger workers to take over for the older ones as they leave the workforce.

However, immigrants have and will continue to contribute much more than that. New business creation is declining as well, except among immigrant populations. Often frozen out of the existing job market by language and cultural barriers, many immigrants start their own businesses. And the more successful ones wind up providing jobs for others, immigrants and non-immigrants alike. Some of the most successful entrepreneurs in the United States—Sergey Brin of Google, Andy Grove of Intel, Do Won Chang of Forever 21, Gurbaksh Chahal of Gwallett, Pierre Omidyar of eBay, Elon Musk of Tesla, Thai Lee of SHI International, Peggy Cherng of Panda Express, Neerja Sethi of Syntel, Weili Dai of Marvell Technology Group, Jayshree Ullal of Arista Networks, Sachiko Kuno of Sucampo Pharmaceuticals—are immigrants. The only American citizens who could justifiably oppose immigration are the Indians.[8]

Many of the reviled southern Italians and Sicilians, the overwhelming majority of whom were not criminals, became good citizens of their new homeland. Furthermore, as the police and military will attest, the only way to defeat criminal groups embedded in the immigrant population is by obtaining inside intelligence—intelligence that can only be acquired through the cooperation and assistance of others from the same cultural background. This is a lesson that needs to be remembered as we struggle to come to terms with a new type of domestic terror. The immigrants themselves will play a key role in extinguishing it, much as they did when our biggest threat was a circle of blackmailers who called themselves the Society of the Banana.

—David Meyers

# 1
# A RATHER GOOD THING

*When the law is powerless, the rights delegated by the people are relegated back to them and they are justified in doing what the courts have failed to do.*[9]
—*William S. Parkerson*

Shortly after eleven o'clock on the evening of October 15, 1890, Chief of Police David C. Hennessy left his office at the Central Police Station, accompanied by his friend Captain Bill O'Connor of the Boyland Detective Agency. It was a humid night in New Orleans. There had been a heavy rain earlier, and a thick mist hung in the air.

A bachelor who lived with his elderly mother, Chief Hennessy was accustomed to putting in long hours. While he seldom ventured out alone anymore owing to numerous death threats, he still had a passion for keeping a watchful eye on the shadowy courts and alleys of his city. He also had a lot on his mind. The truce he had orchestrated between two rival factions—the Provenzanos and the Matrangas—had fallen apart, culminating in a deadly skirmish. The Provenzano gang had been found guilty. However, the men would be retried in four days, and it was rumored that Hennessy's testimony would overturn their convictions.

As the two men neared the chief's residence, they parted ways and the chief continued on alone. Hennessy had ventured no more than a block and a half when he was cut down by a fusillade of bullets fired from a nearby shoemaker's shack. Just moments before, a boy had run by him and whistled. That had been the signal for the attack. Only thirty-two years old,

The Provenzanos and the Matrangas battled for control of the New Orleans waterfront. *Library of Congress.*

Hennessy still exhibited the bravado of youth, despite the assassination of his own father nearly two decades before. Now, as slugs ripped into his face, neck, arms and legs, he struggled to squeeze off several shots from his own revolver as his assailants dispersed.

As soon as the gunfire erupted, O'Connor had rushed to his friend's side. He found Hennessy crumpled on the wet pavement. Gravely wounded, Hennessy managed to whisper, "Dagoes did it."[10] He repeated this accusation at the Charity Hospital, where he died ten hours later. By then, the police had found five discarded weapons a couple of blocks from the crime scene. One was a standard double-barreled shotgun. "The others were curious pieces—shotguns with the barrels sawed off and the stocks hinged so that the guns could be collapsed to the size of a horse pistol and easily concealed"—assassins' weapons.[11]

Hennessy's murder was attributed to a longstanding conflict between two rival produce dealers, Giuseppe "Joseph" Provenzano and Carlo "Charles" Matranga. Provenzano had once controlled the right to unload the ships bringing fruit to New Orleans, but Matranga eventually persuaded or coerced the local merchants into granting him the monopoly. As a result, Provenzano was purportedly out for blood. On May 6, 1890, his men were thought to have attacked a half dozen longshoremen who worked for Matranga. In the ensuing gun battle, gang members were killed or wounded on both sides.

Although a half dozen of Provenzano's men were convicted of attempted murder, they were immediately granted a new trial. Hennessy, a personal friend of the Provenzanos, believed that Matranga had been importing Italian and Sicilian criminals into New Orleans and that as many as one hundred were already working on the docks. In a city of a quarter of a million, the Italian consulate estimated that over one thousand of the city's twenty-five thousand Italians were fugitives from justice in their home country.

"Matranga was described as having been the head of the dreaded Mafia, or Stoppaghera, society in New Orleans," according to the *New York Times*.[12] The word *Mafia* had first appeared in the title of Giuseppe Rizzuto's 1863 play *I Mafiusi di la Vicaria* (*The Mafiosi of the Vicaria*). The story concerned a gang of inmates in Vicaria Prison who extorted money and various favors from the other prisoners. However, the meaning of the term was left unexplained.

David Hennessy's rapid ascent to the position of police chief was the stuff of legends. While still a teenager, he had surprised two local thugs in the act of committing a theft and administered a beating with his bare hands before hauling them off to the police station. He subsequently joined the city police force at the age of seventeen and made detective three years later. In 1881, he assisted in the capture of Sicilian fugitive Giuseppe Esposito.

An international criminal wanted for murder, Esposito arrived in New Orleans in 1879. Not long afterward, he began carving out a niche for himself on the local waterfront, supported by second in command Joe Provenzano. Using the aliases Vincenzo Rebello or Giuseppe Randazzo, Esposito gathered a "band of seventy-five cut-throats" and set about kidnapping other Italians for ransom.[13] The faction, known as the Giardinieri, soon dominated racketeering on the docks and especially among local produce dealers. An informer, Tony Labruzzo, tipped New Orleans police to Esposito's true identity, prompting his arrest by David Hennessy, Michael Hennessy (a cousin) and others. Deported to Italy on September 21, 1881, to stand trial for murder, Esposito received a life sentence.

"Esposito was correctly described in the New Orleans press as 'Esposito, The Bandit,' 'Bold Brigand,'" wrote historian John V. Baiamonte Jr., "but at no time was Esposito described as a Mafia chieftain by the press and others as he would be in later years."[14] After Esposito was taken into custody, however, David Hennessy was allegedly offered a bribe of $30,000 to $50,000 to turn him loose. In the void left by Esposito's absence, his

In 1890, Police Chief David Hennessy of New Orleans was assassinated. *Authors' collection.*

New Orleans criminal organization purportedly broke into two families: the Stoppagghieri led by the Matrangas and the Giardinieri led by the Provenzanos.

As many writers have pointed out, there are two camps regarding Giuseppe Esposito: either he was a true Mafioso or he was no more than a bandit. According to an FBI report, Esposito "was the first known Sicilian Mafia member to emigrate [*sic*] to the United States. He and six other Sicilians fled to New York after murdering eleven wealthy landowners, the chancellor and vice chancellor of a Sicilian province."[15]

Based on his role in taking Esposito down, David Hennessy fully expected to be appointed chief of detectives. When he wasn't, he left the force. Moving into private police work, he quickly became the most formidable law enforcement officer in the city. Mayor Joseph A. Shakspeare subsequently asked him to rejoin the force in 1889—as chief of police. By no means, however, was Hennessy a white knight. He was rumored to have a business interest in several houses of prostitution in Storyville, the city's legendary red-light district. And his alleged partners were Joe and Peter Provenzano. Also, Hennessy had been tried (but acquitted) for the murder of Thomas Devereaux, the city's late chief of detectives.[16]

The argument against the Matranga brothers' supposed Mafia connection begins with the fact that, contrary to the Sicilian code of *omerta* (silence), they openly blamed the Provenzanos for the ambush. Also in violation of the code, they pursued the matter in court. Although the local press branded the shooting a Mafia crime, law enforcement came to view it as simply another vendetta case—something else that had been brought over from "the old country." And for this the Provenzanos were found guilty.

Acting on Mayor Shakspeare's orders, the police had swept through the surrounding neighborhoods and rounded up dozens of Italians, charging some forty-five or fifty with complicity in Hennessy's death. "Any Italian carrying a gun, which was not uncommon for citizens of New Orleans during this period, was quickly arrested," Baiamonte wrote.[17] The Italian community was outraged, not only by the murder but also by the treatment they were accorded. The *Daily States* printed that the killers were "a villainous looking set, with low, receding brows, furtive eyes and that undeniable air about them betraying the low, brutal disposition of a certain class of men. They are not Italians, but Sicilians."[18] And by Sicilians, they meant bandits.[19] Their guilt was presumed.

Due to his friendship with the late police chief, William A. Pinkerton volunteered the assistance of the Pinkerton Detective Agency in the investigation of Hennessy's murder.[20] In early January 1891, one of his best agents and a specialist in Italian crime, Frances P. "Frank" Dimaio, traveled to Amite City, Louisiana, masquerading as counterfeiter Anthony Ruggerio (an actual criminal who was imprisoned in Italy at the time). Dimaio carried $6,000 in phony bills, either in a valise or sewn into the lining of his coat. A short, muscular man who would pick up the nickname "The Raven," Dimaio spoke several languages, including Sicilian. His true identity was a closely held secret known only to four Pinkertons, the head of the Secret Service and the New Orleans district attorney.

Working in concert with the Pinkertons and New Orleans officials, the U.S. Secret Service made a great display of arresting "Ruggerio" at a local boardinghouse. Dimaio played the part of a belligerent criminal so well that an attempt was made to lynch him. Fortunately, a Secret Service agent was able to wrangle him on board the train to New Orleans. Upon arrival, he was placed in a parish prison cell with one of the nineteen defendants in the Hennessy murder—either Pietro Monasterio or Emmanuelle "Joe" Polizi (or Polizzi). A street vendor, Polizi had a scrape in Austin, Texas, a couple of years earlier in which he allegedly cut a man. Monasterio was the shoemaker who occupied the shack from which the shots had been fired.

Over the next several months, Dimaio endeavored to befriend his cellmate in order to learn what he could about the planning of Hennessy's assassination. Polizi or Monasterio may or may not (sources differ) have fingered Charles Matranga and Joe Macheca as the ringleaders. While incarcerated, Dimaio lost forty pounds after contracting dysentery and malaria. Following his release in late March, he would require more than a year to recuperate.

"Hennessy regarded Macheca as a bad man," newspapers reported. "He was once the captain of the Innocents, a Sicilian political body charged with many dark crimes."[21] His threat to expose Macheca was also thought to be a reason for his death. Hennessy had purportedly received a letter warning him that he would be attacked at the window of his office or on his way home. However, allegations that Hennessy was killed in retribution for his arrest of Esposito seem far-fetched, given that nine years had passed.

There was already considerable anti-Italian sentiment in New Orleans and the nation, as exemplified by a contemporary article in *Popular Science Monthly* titled, "What Shall We Do with the Dago?"[22] Of the nearly four dozen Italians rounded up by police, nineteen—described as Mafia members by the newspapers—were indicted for Hennessy's murder. Most of them could be tied directly to Matranga. The city was worked up into such a frenzy over the affair that the son of a prominent businessman walked into the city prison on the day of Hennessy's funeral and shot one of the suspects in the neck. The gunman was sentenced to six months in jail.

At their retrial in January, the Provenzanos were found not guilty of the attack upon the Matrangas, even without the testimony of the martyred police chief. Clearly, the citizens of New Orleans had picked sides. Nine of Hennessy's alleged killers went on trial on February 16, 1891, represented by a formidable team of attorneys. As the *New York Times* noted, Italians throughout the country had contributed more than $75,000 for their defense.

The press and the public still believed the police chief had been slain by the Mafia, but the judge refused to allow the term to be used during the trial. Although many people had witnessed the shooters fleeing the scene, none of them was able to identify the suspects. "Finally, [Joe Polizi] offered in the judge's chambers a bizarre confession of the murder and a description of the inner workings of the Mafia."[23] Both the judge and the district attorney dismissed his story as the ravings of an emotionally disturbed individual.

Testimony established that Macheca had rented the shack from which the shots were fired under the name of "Peter Johnson." He then moved Monasterio, a make-believe shoemaker, into it shortly before the assassination took place. An eyewitness had watched Antonio Scaffidi, Bastian Incardona and Antonio Bagnetto firing at Hennessy from in front of the shack. Fourteen-year-old Caspare Marchesi, son of Antonio Marchesi, had confided to another youth that he had been stationed as the lookout on the night of the murder and notified the others when the police chief was approaching. However, defense witnesses placed Bagnetto, the Marchesis (father and son) and Scaffidi elsewhere at the time of the ambush.

The jurors took a day to weigh the evidence. Machea, Matranga, Bagnetto, Incardona and the two Marchesis were found not guilty, while a mistrial was declared for the remaining three. Nearly all of the spectators and much of the community were outraged by the decision. The reporter for the *New York Times* wrote, "So strong a case had been made by the State, the evidence

The Committee of Fifty, led by William Parkerson, raised a mob to lynch Hennessy's killers. *Authors' collection.*

had been so clear, direct and unchallenged, that the acquittal of the accused today came like a thunder clap from a clear sky."[24] Word on the street was that the jurors had been bribed. Meanwhile, the nine defendants were returned to their cells to await trial on lesser charges. They joined the ten other men who had yet to have their day in court. However, it was believed that all charges would be dismissed within a few days.

In the aftermath of Hennessy's assassination, Mayor Shakspeare was making incendiary speeches, blaming the police chief's death on "Sicilian vengeance" and calling on the citizens of New Orleans to "teach these people a lesson they will never forget."[25] Shakspeare appointed a Committee of Fifty, drawn from the ranks of prominent members of the community, to devise a plan for eradicating the city's secret criminal societies, assuming there were any. Dismayed by the trial's outcome, the committee retired to the office of attorney William S. Parkerson that same afternoon. Many of them were also members of the Anti-Lottery League, a group that opposed the renewal of the Louisiana State Lottery Company's charter out of concerns that it attracted too many Italians to New Orleans. They promptly called for a public meeting that same evening at ten o'clock. This time they were joined by a mob of six to eight thousand.

Fired up by speeches from the Committee of Fifty and led by Parkerson, the mob began marching on the parish prison. By the time they reached the lockup, their numbers had increased from twelve thousand to as many as twenty thousand. In short order, they stormed the block-long fortress, shot nine of the Matranga gang (some of whom had yet to be tried) and hanged

21

two others (one of whom was likely already dead). They spared Caspare Marchesi because of his youth, while Matranga and Incardona somehow hid themselves and escaped detection.

The lynch mob was roundly praised by the chamber of commerce and others for its actions. A grand jury refused to indict any of them, noting that the mob "embraced several thousand of the first, best and even the most law-abiding citizens of the city....[I]n fact, the act seemed to involve the entire people of the parish and the City of New Orleans."[26] Theodore Roosevelt, just three years away from becoming president of the United States, said of the lynching that it was "a rather good thing."[27] Justice may not have been served, but Hennessy's death had been avenged in a way that the underworld could understand.

In the days that followed, Dexter S. Gaster, newly appointed superintendent of police, compiled a list of ninety-four murders and affrays committed by Sicilians and Italians in New Orleans between 1866 and 1891.[28] Plagued with errors, Gaster's "research" confirmed what he already believed in his heart—that the Mafia was real and that it intended to take over the city after first killing him and the mayor.

Ultimately, no indictments were returned against the leaders of the lynch mob or against Hennessy's killers, although at least a few of them were thought to be among the unmourned dead. However, nearly twenty years later, an attempt would be made to pin the police chief's killing on a couple of toughs in Ohio.

# 2

# WIDE OPEN AND UNGUARDED

[Italians are] *just a little worse than the Negro,*
*being if anything filthier in their habits, lawless, and treacherous.*[29]
*—John M. Parker*

J ohn Parker, a Progressive Democrat who later became governor
of Louisiana, never felt a need to apologize. As an organizer of the
mob that avenged the murder of Chief Hennessy, Parker believed
that the summary execution of eleven Italian prisoners was justified.
And his good friend (and idol) Teddy Roosevelt agreed. In her doctoral
dissertation, Barbara Obtain concluded that the Hennessy case "created a
very negative and enduring image of Italian immigrants in the American
mind."[30] Sicilians came to be regarded as a primitive people, ruled by
passion, prone to violence and disposed toward criminality. Parker helped
to stoke that fire.

During the period between Hennessy's slaying and the start of
Prohibition, "no aspect of Italian immigrant activity received so much
attention or excited the interest of the American public as greatly as
did crime."[31] Threatening letters, kidnappings, bombings or otherwise
unexplained murders were increasingly attributed to a nebulous Black
Hand Society. Extortion attempts, in particular, came to be viewed as the
most typically Italian of all crimes.

More than four million Italians came to the United States between 1880
and 1920, the majority between 1900 and 1917. No other ethnic group

A wistful vista of Calabria, the southern "toe" of the Italian peninsula. *Authors' collection.*

contributed as many immigrants in such a brief span of time. They were primarily males aged twenty-five to forty-five, and many intended to return home with the money they earned. Others hoped to send for their families once they were established in America. But these hopefuls soon learned that streets were not paved with gold. In fact, between 1901 and 1920, fully 50 percent of Italian immigrants repatriated—returned to Italy.

However, not all who went home to Italy were welcome. One such returnee, said to be worth at least $300, abused the staff of a tavern, knocking one man down for not polishing his boots quickly enough. When confronted by the landlord, he flashed a handful of cash and offered to buy the place. As one reporter observed, "The actions of these vulgar rich are becoming almost unbearable."[32]

By the mid-nineteenth century, the United States had become infected by Native Americanism, a political ideology characterized by hostility toward immigrants ("foreigners") and Roman Catholics ("the system of Popery"). These principles were at the core of many hate groups, including the Know-Nothing Party, the American Protective Association and the Ku Klux Klan. The spirit of nativism can still be seen today in the

24

prejudice displayed toward such immigrant groups as Mexicans, Somalis and Muslims. But in the early years of the next century, the target, like the Germans and Irish before them, was Italians and, among Italians, Sicilians.[33]

Conditions in southern Italy had become steadily worse since 1871, the year in which it finally became a unified and democratic nation. The land had grown poor and infertile due to droughts, heat waves, parasites and soil mismanagement. Most farmers were little better than sharecroppers and had no opportunity for upward mobility. The situation was dire for skilled tradesmen as well. With the economy stuck in the doldrums, there were few jobs to be had, so those seeking employment were forced to look outside the country—to America.

Many Italian immigrants fell victim to the *padrone* or contract labor system. The padroni, or employment agents, would recruit immigrants to work as longshoremen, miners and railroaders or in other forms of hard labor. Often working on commission, the padrone would serve as an intermediary between the employer and employee, lining up the immigrant with a job and lodging. However, the padrone also was in a position to exploit the worker by hiring him out as a strikebreaker or wage cutter.

There were also instances in which these flesh peddlers brought the immigrants from southern Italy and crammed them into tenements with as many as twenty people—men, women, boys and girls—living in a two-bedroom apartment just twelve feet square. For his efforts, the padrone might keep 60 percent or more of the workers' pay. The system benefitted from the fact that most Italian immigrants did not speak English and were wary of living in a large city apart from others like themselves. So they tended to settle in colonies. However, as more and more immigrants picked up the language and learned the culture, they became increasingly independent and the padroni's influence diminished. World War I finally put an end to it.

Thomas Bailey Aldrich, novelist, poet, editor of the *Atlantic Monthly* and friend of Mark Twain (who called him "the sincerest man who walks"), was a raging xenophobe who held many immigrants in low regard. In his poem "Unguarded Gates," he warned, "Wide open and unguarded stand our gates, And through them presses a wild motley throng." Aldrich railed against their "unknown gods and rites," "tiger passions," "strange tongues" and "accents of menace," all the while defending his stance with the assertion, "I believe in America for Americans."[34] It was the very antithesis of the Emma Lazarus sonnet inscribed on the base of the Statue of Liberty.

Thomas Bailey Aldrich was the respected, but xenophobic, editor of the *Atlantic Monthly*. *Library of Congress.*

In some cases, the immigrants had been thugs and highwaymen in their homeland and were put on boats to the United States by Italian authorities eager to be rid of them. Once here, some resumed their criminal ways. But that was the exception. And the challenges they faced have changed little over the years. They needed to find housing. They needed to secure work. They needed to learn the language and the customs of the land.

In New York, Italian immigrants were blamed, even by mission workers, for the squalor in which they lived. Somehow, they were held accountable for the fact that so many of them occupied such small quarters. They were described as being dirtier than other nationalities. And they worked in menial, poorly paid jobs. When compared to the Chinese, they purportedly kept less of the money they earned, sending the lion's share back to family in Italy.

Many immigrants were accustomed to fresh fruit in their diet. Upon coming to America, they discovered that the fruit trade was not well developed, so they set about improving the situation. Soon, fruit stands began popping up in towns throughout the United States, operated primarily by Italians and Greeks. Peddlers emerged, pushing carts up and down the streets in competition with organ grinders and the popcorn, peanut and taffy salesmen—immigrants all.

Disdain for Italians was common during this period. In an 1887 article on immigration, it was reported that Italy "sends us, every thirty days, 2,334 organ grinders and banana peddlers."[35] They were considered rude, aggressive, dishonest, dangerous and unclean. While many of them did have a shabby and forlorn appearance, the banana peddlers, as they were called, were often shrewd businessmen who often turned a tidy profit, albeit by putting in long hours. But that did not buy them respect. A typical joke of the period went like this: "A banana peddler said once, 'Some days I do nothing and other days I do twice as much.'"[36]

These vendors purchased unripe fruit from commission houses or importers at wholesale prices. They would then store them in rented cellars until they had ripened sufficiently to be sold at a price that earned them a reasonable profit. Any produce that failed to sell would be consumed by the peddler and his family so the brown bananas and other blemished fruits and vegetables did not go to waste. Many of these street vendors were able to save enough money over time to become commission agents or importers themselves.

The public perception of banana peddlers was captured in Frank Dumont's song "The Dagoe Banana Peddler." Published in 1888 by Willis Woodward & Company of New York, it included the lyric, "My fadder you know was a brigand. / But he was hung by de neck, / I always have my good stiletto, / Where de police can never suspect."

Italians were notorious for carrying stilettos, a cross-shaped dagger with a tapered blade and a needle-like point. It was a weapon designed for stabbing and often did not have sharpened edges. Used primarily for self-defense, it became particularly popular among gamblers, gang members and other ne'er-do-wells. In New Orleans, stilettos figured in so many stabbings and murders that an ordinance was passed in 1879 banning them from being sold or exhibited for sale within the limits of the city. It soon gave way to the clasp knife.

Depending on whether they were skilled or unskilled, Italian immigrants sought positions as tailors, shoemakers, laborers, sweatshop workers, music teachers or vendors. They were also well represented in the mines, textile mills and clothing factories. Many of those who settled in Columbus worked for the railroads, the stone quarries or the fruit trade.

Apprehension about foreigners was not new. Benjamin Franklin had expressed concern that the influx of German immigrants would undermine America's culture—British culture, that is.[37] "Why should Pennsylvania," he asked, "founded by the English, become a Colony of Aliens, who will shortly be so numerous as to Germanize us, instead of our Anglifying them."[38] By the mid-1880s, Irish immigrants, especially Catholics, were regarded as worthless drunks, averse to work and quick to fight. An article in *Harper's Weekly* asserted, "They have so behaved themselves that nearly seventy-five per cent of our criminals and paupers are Irish; that fully seventy-five per cent of the crimes of violence committed among us are the work of Irishmen."[39] However, few would argue today that the Germans and Irish have failed to assimilate into the American culture.

At the beginning of the twentieth century, "Many scholars believed that Southern and Central European 'races' were genetically inferior to the Northern and Western European groups who had emigrated to the United States in earlier times and had defined American culture."[40] A Harvard University economics professor, William Z. Ripley, went so far as to take out a full-page ad in the *New York Times* in which he warned that "the hordes of new immigrants" were "a menace to our Anglo Saxon civilization."[41] Then there was Woodrow Wilson.

In his five-volume *A History of the American People*, Wilson wrote that the sturdy European stocks were being replaced by "men of the lowest class from the south of Italy and men of the meaner sort out of Hungary and Poland."[42] He charged that they were lazy and stupid, the "more sordid and hapless elements of their population."[43] African Americans and Roman Catholics, in particular, received his scorn.

A leading light in the Progressive Movement, Wilson was elected the country's twenty-eighth president on the Democratic ticket and helped to craft the 1924 Immigration Act. By imposing a quota system using the

A typical back alley scene at a tenement house in New York's Italian quarter. *Authors' collection.*

1890 census as a baseline, this piece of legislation favored immigrants from northern and western Europe to the detriment of those from southern and eastern Europe, Asia and Africa. But until then, the "lowest class" of Italians continued to stream through America's unguarded gates.

Frank White Marshall wrote in *Pearson's Magazine* that by 1906, there were "five thousand Italian criminals, ex-convicts and desperadoes, Sicilians and Calabrians" in the city of New York who "lived by robbery and extortion, frequently accompanied by murder, their victims being confined entirely to the more honest and industrious of their own race."[44] Three years later, the bias against foreigners was quite pronounced within the Irish-dominated law enforcement community of New York City and, by extension, everywhere else.

Although the New York police believed an overwhelming number of criminals were foreigners, an analysis of court records in Manhattan and the Bronx for the years 1904–7 revealed that nearly 65 percent of the individuals convicted of "high crimes" in the court of general sessions proved to be native born. Only 8.4 percent were Italians.

Francis Oppenheimer, author of "The Truth About the Black Hand," accused the police of branding everyone a criminal who was brought into the station. "This included the poor immigrant who may keep a pushcart without a license and an illiterate 'son of sunny Italy' who might perhaps have thrown some peelings on the walk or stuffed newspapers in the wrong barrel."[45] Roughly a quarter of the 200,000 persons arrested in 1907 were charged with such minor offenses as breaking windows or playing ball. Superintendent Wallace Gillpatrick of the Chrystie Street House, a temporary shelter for young men and boys, asserted that it was a crime in New York City "for a boy to be penniless and without a home."[46] He could have added "and an immigrant."

## 3

# SEEDS OF THE MAFFIA

*These Sicilians or banana peddlers are the head of it.*[47]
*—Victor P. Churches*

ennessy had been five years in the grave, but law enforcement throughout the country was still divided on the question of whether the Mafia had set up shop in New Orleans or anywhere else for that matter. As waves of Italian immigrants poured into the United States, crime by and against Italians flourished. While many Italian criminals had collected in New Orleans, New York and Chicago, they didn't necessarily stay there. At least one made his way to Columbus, Ohio.

Oscar Durante, editor of the Chicago daily *l'Italia*, received two letters from a Freda Thornton, 50 North Grubb Street, Columbus. The first, dated November 15, 1891, read:

> *Mr. Oscar Durante, Unknown Friend:*
>
> *No doubt you will be greatly surprised in receiving this letter from me, but having seen you at the World's Fair when I was there a year ago, I fell dead in love with you at first sight and have no peace of mind since I seen [sic] you. It was by chance I discovered your name and address and if you have no objection would like the pleasure of your correspondence.*[48]

At the beginning of the twentieth century, Columbus was known as the Arch City. *Library of Congress.*

Thornton provided Durante with a physical description and mentioned that she expected "to fall heir to a fortune some day."[49] When he failed to reply, she sent him a second letter—in which she professed her continuing love for him—and promised to provide a photo.

Months passed. Then a third letter arrived from a man calling himself Giuseppe Mantello, urging Durante to come to Ohio in order to drum up new subscribers for his newspaper. It was dated October 1894 but mailed in January 1895. Suspecting that it was a ploy by a branch of the Mafia to lure him to his death, Durante wrote a letter of his own—to the Columbus police.

At age twenty-five, Durante was already a prominent member of Chicago's Italian community. He had founded his Italian-language newspaper nine years earlier and would continue to publish it for more than half a century. The king of Italy would knight him for his work in promoting positive relations between their two countries. In the words of the *Chicago Daily News*, "Durante has always worked for the benefit of the Italians in Chicago."[50] However, it hadn't been easy.

A year earlier, Durante had left journalism—briefly, as it turned out—to focus on practicing law after concluding that the majority of Italians being sentenced in court were being punished more for their ignorance and lack of education than their criminality. In two capital cases, he succeeded in having Dominick Corrello's sentence commuted to eight years' imprisonment and Dominick Migliavesi's to three. Both men would have surely been hanged if it had not been for Durante's advocacy.

However, at the October 6, 1894 meeting of the McKinley Club in Chicago, a man named Raeffael De Bartolo brushed past the doorkeeper, shouting something about Black Hand vengeance. Drawing a gun, he fired at Durante. The shot whizzed by his head. De Bartolo was supposedly angry with Durante for attempting to swing Italian voters away from the Democratic Party.[51]

After corresponding with Durante, Columbus chief of police Edward Pagles wondered whether "seeds of the Maffia [sic] were being sown" in Columbus.[52] A former ticket agent for the Big Four Railroad, Pagles had run for mayor on the Republican ticket. It was expected that his fellow railroad workers would sweep him into office. When Democrat George J. Karb won instead, Pagles was installed as police chief in June 1893, replacing John E. Murphy, who had passed away five months earlier.

Columbus had been settled by largely English-speaking people, including a few free blacks. Later, throngs of immigrants began to arrive. First there were the Germans, then the Irish and, finally, the Italians. Although there had been Italians in Columbus since John Marzetti took up residence in 1861, most of the immigration occurred in the decades leading up to World War I.[53] As was the case in other communities, few of the immigrants spoke English, and they tended to keep to themselves, forming tightknit (and tight-lipped) little colonies or settlements. Most Italians were law-abiding, but there was a faction that formed neighborhood gangs to prey on other Italian immigrants.

Chief Pagles assigned Italian-born Victor P. Churches to investigate. Along with Peter Albanese and Joseph L. Schiavo, Churches would form the department's Italian unit, which would prove indispensable in combating the city's budding criminal underworld.[54] Churches quickly rounded up Mantello (aka Mandone) but could not locate Thornton. When he went to the address given for the love-struck woman, he found the prison guard who lived there had never heard of her.

"I am sure that Mandone is the man who wrote the letter," Churches said, "because he is no good."[55] He thought the suspect had attempted to disguise his handwriting. However, Mandone denied it. Recently arrived from Chicago, he claimed to know the person responsible but refused to

The heart of Columbus was the northeast corner of Broad and High Streets. *Library of Congress.*

name him, saying, "Durante is his enemy because he wrote [Mandone] up" in his newspaper.[56] (Durante hadn't.) He then left Columbus for Marietta.

"In regard to this Mafia," Churches concluded, "there is nothing in it yet. I think they will organize it here before long. These Sicilians or banana peddlers are the head of it."[57] This wasn't the first time the fruit vendors had been regarded with suspicion. In 1889, the Columbus police raided Italian quarters along Third Street under orders of the city health officer to investigate the rumor that they were wrapping "filthy" bed clothing around the fruit to hasten its ripening. As Captain C.C. Wilcox darkened their doorway, one fleeing Italian exclaimed, "We no sleepy wiz ze bananas."[58]

The American Mafia—La Cosa Nostra ("Our thing")—is often traced back to Vito Cascioferro (or, alternately, Cascio Ferro). In 1901, he came to the United States from Sicily, where he was wanted for the murder of a banker. "Don Vito," as he was known, remained in New York City for a little more than two years, operating a food import business. After beating a counterfeiting rap in Hackensack, New Jersey, Cascioferro hooked up with the Harlem-based Morello-Lupo Gang.

Likely, the first proper Mafia family in New York was organized in 1892. At its head was Giuseppe "The Clutch Hand" Morello, a native of Corleone, Sicily, aided by three half brothers: Cira, Nicola and Vincenzo "Tiger" Terranova. Morello picked up his nickname due to a one-fingered hand that resembled a claw. Ignacio "the Wolf" Lupo (aka Saietta) was a twenty-two-year-old fugitive, also from Corleone (where he had killed a man named, coincidentally, Salvatore Morello). He married the boss's half sister, Salvatrice Morello, and took on the role of enforcer.

In May 1893, the *New York Times* quoted an Italian-born city official on the surge of violent acts committed by Italian immigrants. While the anonymous source asserted that there were many good people in Naples, Messina or Palermo, where the Mafia and Camorra were headquartered, "These good southern Italians…are more apt to aid their murderous compatriots by keeping silent when their testimony could convict because they have been reared to dread the vengeance of these criminal refugees."[59]

Although they would later merge, the Mafia and Camorra were two distinctly different approaches to organized crime. The Mafia was organized vertically, while the Camorra was organized horizontally. Historically older, the Camorra developed as individual clans, acting more or less independently of one another, so the authority was vested in a number of leaders. The Mafia came along later and introduced more centralized authority in a pyramidal structure. If the Mafia was an army, the Camorra was a bunch of terrorist cells.

In the old country, the Mafia and Camorra threatened people and then collected money from them on the promise they would not carry through with their threats. "Immigrating felons who were not sworn members of the Mafia," historian Michael Newton noted, "observed the trend and soor went into business for themselves. Collectively, those operators became known as the 'Black Hand'—La Mano Nera, in Italian—for the inked-palm symbol used to sing their written threats."[60]

Eight years after the fact, the *Evening World* reported that Black Hand letters first began appearing in New York City in 1896 (five years before the arrival of Cascioferro). The following year, ten Italians who refused to pay the extortionists' demands were murdered and their killers never brought to justice. However, the newspapers paid little attention to these incidents and, apparently, did not associate them with the Black Hand. Yet it must have been a topic of conversation, for in August 1902, New Yorkers learned that rehearsals were underway for *The Black Hand*, a play based on the activities of a Mafia-like organization.

Then came the "Barrel Murder." The lifeless body of Benedetto Madonia was found stuffed in a barrel on East Eleventh Street on the morning of April 14, 1903. This was not the first barrel murder in New York, but it was one of the most sensational. Madonia was lured to New York from Buffalo, ostensibly by the Black Hand, although there was no mention of it at the time. Stabbed to death, his body was packed in a barrel and left on a sidewalk in Avenue D. Speculation was that he had been slain "because

Drawn from the headlines, the comedy-drama "Kidnapped in New York" capitalized on Black Hand fears. *Library of Congress.*

he threatened to expose the secrets of the Mafia band of counterfeiters and blackmailers" to which his brother-in-law, Giuseppe "Joseph" de Priemo (or Primo), belonged.[61]

De Priemo, already imprisoned at Sing Sing, denied any Mafia connection to the killing, but not everyone believed him. One of the investigators working the Mafia angle was New York detective Joe Petrosino. When he showed de Priemo a photo of the dead man, he fainted after admitting it was his brother-in-law. He said he had sent Madonia to meet with the counterfeiters to claim his share of the money. The police believed the band included some twenty or thirty men who were currently serving time in various prisons. As it turned out, Mandonia was also a member of the gang and not on good terms with its leader, Giuseppe Morello. The Morello family's hallmark was disposing of corpses in barrels.

The author of the first Black Hand letter is a fact lost to history, as is when and where it first appeared. The earliest known published use of the term was in September 1903 when the *New York Herald* ran an article titled "'Black Hand' Band in Extortion Plot."[62] It told how Nicola (or Nicolo) Capiello, a successful Brooklyn dock builder, had received a note on August 3, 1903:

*Nicola Capiello,*

*If you don't meet us at Seventy-second Street and Thirteenth Avenue, Brooklyn, to-morrow afternoon, your house will be dynamited and you and your family will be killed. The same fate awaits you in the event of your betraying our purpose to the police.*

*Mano Nera*[63]

Capiello ignored it. Two days later, a second letter arrived:

*You did not meet us as ordered in our first letter. If you still refuse to acede to our terms, but wish to preserve the lives of your family, you can do so by sacrificing your own life. Walk in Sixteenth Street, near Seventh Avenue between the hours of four and five tonite.*

*Beware of Mano Nera*[64]

When Capiello still failed to show up, he received a demand for $10,000. (He was estimated to be worth more than $100,000.) But Capiello was either brave or foolhardy and refused to comply. Not long afterward, three of Capiello's supposed friends presented themselves along with a fourth man he did not know. They volunteered to act as intermediaries, suggesting they could persuade the extortionists to spare him if he paid as little as $1,000.

On August 26, Capiello surrendered $1,000 to the blackmailers. However, a few days later, the four men returned, this time with a letter in a dirty envelope asking him for $3,000 more:

> *We will write you in a day or two to inform you where to deliver this money, and we warn you on pain of death not to have any communication with the police. You will be under our eyes from this time on, and we shall know if you act as an honorable man. Be discreet, for if this letter comes to the knowledge of the police, you and every one of your family will perish by dynamite or the dagger.*[65]

Fearing assassination, Capiello went directly to Captain Charles Formosa and begged for police protection. The letter stated: "I swear to you on my honor that during the month you will be killed. The Black Hand will follow all."[66] Initially, Captain Formosa told the businessman that it was likely a bluff. However, on September 12, he arranged for the arrest of the four men who had been "assisting" Capiello—Mariano Esposito, Fortunato Castellano, Annuziato Lingria (or possibly Amazito Langia) and Biaggio Giordana—plus their behind-scenes confederate, Antonio Giordana. "The arrest of the four men…caused a senation in the President Street Italian quarter."[67] While all five were tried and convicted of extortion, Capiello continued to receive letters from associates of the malefactors.

Another early case—some sources say the first—in which the police were involved was that of Gaetano Riggio, a grocer, who was threatened with death if he did not pay $500. An attempt to trap the blackmailers failed. Although the Black Hand did not make good its threats against Riggio, he and his wife were later murdered in February 1906 by Josephine Terranova, a young woman who had lived with them and claimed he had done "a great wrong" to her when she was thirteen.[68]

Other purported Black Hand crimes included the disappearance of Luigi Castellano, a small banker on Mulberrry Street, who refused to pay $1,000; the similar disappearance of Angelo Peccaro, an Elizabeth Street fruit merchant, who also refused to pay tribute; and the shocking murder of Giuseppi Catania, a Brooklyn grocer whose mutilated body was found in a potato sack in the water off the Bay Bridge after he ignored a threatening letter. This crime was investigated by a newly minted detective sergeant, Anthony F. Vachris.

Charles Bacigalupo, nicknamed the "Mayor of Mulberry Bend" (the Italian district of lower Manhattan), told reporters that the extortionists were "bad people to deal with, and are, I believe, working in all cities in this country where there are Italians colonies."[69] Mulberry Street was where some of the worst tenements were located, and Elizabeth Street, two blocks away, came to be regarded as the center of Black Hand operations.

Inspector George W. McClusky, Detective Petrosino's supervisor, admitted that the Black Hand was at work in New York City. "I know of one Italian doctor in this city who gave up $400 on the receipt of a letter, and it is likely that he will have to give up $1,000 because he yielded once."[70] However, McClusky added, "In all my experience there has not been a murder of any kind that could possibly be laid at the door of this crowd. If it wasn't for the refusal of the Italians to aid the police this gang could be wiped out in forty-eight hours."[71]

The same month, Nicholas Parella, a Brooklyn resident, disappeared on his way to work, "following threats of assassination by the Black Hand Society."[72] He had lodged earlier complaints against four Italians, presumably for blackmailing him. The police suspected he had been kidnapped. At about the same time, Salvator Especiale, "a refined and cultured man, supposed to have been a secret agent of the Government working to detect counterfeiters," was found murdered in front of what was believed to have been a counterfeiters' den in New York City.[73] Two men were arrested, one with a bullet wound in his shoulder, thought to have been received in an exchange of gunfire with the dead man.

By December 1903, the New York Police Department had forty letters in its possession written by agents of the Black Hand, demanding payment from Italian residents of the city. There was a veritable reign of terror in the Italian community, especially among the well-to-do. And it was just beginning.

**4**

# ALIVE IF YOU CAN

*The appearance of the Black Hand in New York is no dream
of yellow journalism, no illusion of an excited group.
The Black Hand has actually appeared.*[74]
—Barbour County Index

B y the early twentieth century, most large cities in the United States had nascent ties to Mafia or Mafia-like organizations. Charles Matranga, who had barely escaped being lynched, would within a few years become the undisputed chief of the New Orleans underworld. Giacomo "Big Jim" Colosimo, who came to Chicago from Calabria, Italy, soon took control of the city's illicit scene, allying himself with the six Genna brothers, who used the Unione Siciliana as a front for their criminal enterprise. And Giuseppe Morello and his kin would develop business relationships with the Mafiosi in both Chicago and New Orleans.

Despite the fact that 10 percent of the population of New York City was Italian by 1904, there were only 7 Italian police officers and 1 detective in a force of over 8,100. The detective's name was Giuseppe "Joe" Petrosino. Born in Padula, Italy, he joined the New York Police Department in 1883, where his fluency in several Italian dialects came in handy. When Theodore Roosevelt became a police commissioner, he took notice of Petrosino and promoted him to detective sergeant in charge of the homicide bureau. His unique qualifications resulted in his being called on to investigate many alleged Black Hand crimes.

Unloading bananas at the bustling waterfront in New York City. *Library of Congress.*

One of the earliest of these occurred in January 1902. A small band of criminals calling themselves "Holy House" attempted to blackmail Stephen Carmenciti, a well-to-do New York tailor. Detective Petrosino persuaded Carmenciti to meet with the extortionists and pay them the $150 they demanded. He then arrested Joseph Mascarello and Carmine Mursunesco. However, the case fell apart when the tailor refused to testify against them for fear of retribution.

Giuseppe Giordana, a Brooklyn grocer, received a Black Hand letter on January 16, 1904. Signed "A.B.C.," it ordered him to take $500 to "Sixth Street and the river," where someone would meet him.[75] The police were puzzled, however, because there was no such location. Over in Newark, New Jersey, contractor Michael Rosetti was the recipient of a Black Hand letter in February, demanding $400 or else he and his wife would die. Written in Italian, it concluded with the warning, "Fail us not."[76] The police provided Rosetti with $400 so he could make the drop, but no one showed up to collect it.

New Yorker Cologne Decaneine received a Black Hand letter written in red ink on March 7 and took it directly to the East Thirty-Fifth Street police station. The letter directed him to meet a member of the "society" at the Brooklyn Bridge with $100 in cash. Otherwise, "If you do not keep the appointment prepare for death within ten days."[77] The letter was embellished with doodles of daggers, pistols, skulls and crossed bones. Undoubtedly, there were many more blackmail letters the police did not know about.

When threats proved ineffective, bombings commenced. As the *New York Times* reported, "A dynamite bomb or infernal machine which had been put in the doorway of Poggrioriale [likely Poggioreale] Ciro's grocery store" exploded early on the morning of July 29, propelling the owner and his wife out of their bed.[78] Ciro acknowledged that he had received a series of Black Hand letters. Six days earlier, he had received a letter instructing him to meet the author at the end of the Third Avenue elevated railroad on the night of July 28 with $2,000 in cash. Instead, he handed the letter over to the police.

Captain Mertens said that since he had been in command of the Mulberry Street Station at least fifty similar cases had been brought to his attention. However, he did not anticipate solving them because "the Italians of all classes are in such mortal terror of the blackmailers that they do not dare to give the police any assistance whatever for fear that they will be marked for vengeance and murder."[79] Ciro refused to name the men he suspected. "Me speaks no more," the grocer was quoted as saying by the *New York Times*. "Me shutta up. Suppose I tell they give me da stillett [*sic*]."[80]

A bomb was thrown into a crowd on Saturday night, August 6, during an Italian picnic on East 151st Street in New York. Peter Dimerio (or Dimico or Demerio) was running a bar in the middle of a vacant lot when Vincenzio Donnetto (or Donetto) walked up to it at about nine o'clock and demanded money. "Demerio refused to give him any, whereupon Donnetto moved back about ten feet and, drawing a bomb from his pocket, threw it at a barrel in front of the stand."[81] Twenty persons were injured, including Donnetto—"one leg being badly torn from the hip to the ankle, but he managed to escape at the time and was arrested later at his home."[82] Although he threatened suicide, the police broke down the door to his home before he could reach a weapon. The police suspected he was a member of the Black Hand.

The bombing arose out of a dispute between two saloonkeepers, Giovanni Finnelli and Giovanni Belelo. When Finnelli's rent was raised, he refused to pay and Belelo took over the operation of the saloon. In retaliation, Finnelli began building a rival saloon across the street. Although he had yet to erect

Lieutenant Joseph Petrosino was the public face of the battle with Italian crime. *Library of Congress.*

the walls, Finnelli ordered several barrels of beer and gave away free drinks. Very quickly, some two hundred people had assembled on the lot.

Taking the bait, Belelo sent his men over to Finnelli's and extended invitations for free beer at his place. By now, there were about six hundred Italians milling about. Half were Belelo's friends and half Finnelli's. Several quarrels broke out between the factions in the time leading up to Donnetto's setting off the bomb.

Not long after the bombings started, the extortionists added kidnapping to their bag of tricks. On August 9, eight-year-old Antonio Mannino, son of a wealthy Italian contractor, was abducted and held for a ransom, which quickly jumped from an initial $500 to $50,000. The wife of Francesco Coneglio, the supposed head of the Black Hand in New York, was arrested and taken to jail for questioning. A half dozen detectives were already scouring the city for a handful of Italians who had been suspects in the barrel murder. The police believed they likely knew something about the Mannino kidnapping as well.

On August 12, after two days of questioning, Angelo Cucozza, age eighteen, confessed to Captain Rooney at the Amity Street Station that he had been paid two dollars to lure the child from his home. His admission was prompted by the discovery of some letters and papers in a trunk owned by Antonio Galieri (or Galici) in the room Cucozza had shared with his uncle, Alavarero Sano. When confronted with the incriminating documents, Cucozza broke down. Desperate for money to pay his passage back to Italy, he said he was drawn into the plot a week before the boy was abducted and only after obtaining the consent of his uncle.

Every day for a week, Cucozza met with the man and, the day before the boy was taken, was introduced to Vincenzo "Doe." Doe was the man who guided him to Manhattan after he had lured Tony away from his parents' home. In the view of the police, Doe was the ringleader of the Brooklyn gang, but the real leader was someone who had played a key role in the barrel murder. Sergeant Petrosino ordered "Don Vito" Cascioferro picked up on suspicion, blocking his application for American citizenship. However, Cascioferro had made his way down to New Orleans and, in September 1904, returned to Sicily.

Another warrant was issued for Vito Laduca, who had been arrested several months previously in connection with the murder of Bendetto Madonia, whose mutilated body was found packed in a barrel. In issuing the warrants, Magistrate Tighe said, "Go out and make arrests—alive if you can, dead if you must. The time has come when these men must be taught by getting the full penalty of the law."[83]

One place the police were keeping an eye on was the butcher shop where the victim of the barrel murder was last seen alive. Laduca had formerly lived there, but the police were told he had taken a train for Pittsburgh.[84] The detectives were also trying to track down Cucozza's uncle, who had escaped out of the window of his tenement room while the police were questioning the other tenants. After the suspects were arrested, their friends collected money for their defense from wealthy Italians, including the father of the kidnapped boy. He purportedly refused to believe they had anything to do with the disappearance of his son. Galieri was soon arrested, charged with kidnapping and held on $3,000 bail.

The same day as Cucozza's confession, Antonio Mannino's parents received another letter, rumored to have been mailed from Hoboken, New Jersey. Although the police denied it, they believed he was either being held there or in the Italian section of Manhattan. The boy's father insisted that he expected to have his son back by the end of the week. "And I will not pay any ransom for his return, either," he declared. "I will have my boy back, and when I get him I will not bother about any prosecution."[85]

At four o'clock in the afternoon on August 15, five Italians disembarked from a New York Central train at Fishkill Landing and then jumped aboard a trolley car. When they returned to the station a short time afterward, they had a boy with them. "So suspicious did they appear that it was thought that the boy might be Antonio. He was poorly clad and seemed to be bewildered."[86] According to those who witnessed it, the men bought the boy a sandwich, although he did not seem to regard any of them as a friend. So, one of the witnesses placed a telephone call to Chief of Police Mara. By the time Mara reached the station, the Italians had left. Two of them went to Newburg, New York, while the remaining three took the boy to Camelot, a community above Fishkill Landing where there was an Italian colony. As it turned out, the boy was restored to his parents on the evening of August 18, "having been found alone wandering on the street four blocks from his own home by one of his relatives."[87]

Ruggiero Nicosia, a New York barber, was sent a letter warning him to hand over $4,000. If he did, he and his family would be protected from death at the hands of Fillippo (or Phillippo) and Giuseppe Massano. "When Nicosia received the letter he notified the police. Detective Sergeants Petrosino and Bonnoil were put on the case. Under their instructions Nicoisa [sic] pretended to deal with the 'Black Hand'."[88]

Massano, age thirty-two, entered Nicosia's barbershop, hand on hip as though packing a gun. He told Nicosia the Black Hand had two bombs and would blow up his shop unless he paid them the money. Nicosia said he would give him $125 of the money in the hallway of a tenement house next door to his shop. As detectives watched, the barber handed Massano $125 in marked bills; then they jumped out and captured the suspect. His brother, Fillippo, age twenty-three, was also arrested back at the rooms they shared. The two Sicilian tailors, who had lived in the United States for less than a year, were subsequently "locked up at police headquarters…on a charge of extortion."[89]

John Bologna was given a choice: either pay $100 in blackmail by Monday or he and his son would be blown up. So on August 13, 1904, he went to the Thirty-Fifth Street Police Station to ask for help. He told Captain Shires that he had met a man whose name he didn't remember about a year ago. The day before, he had run into him in the street while on his way to visit a friend. Grabbing him by the lapel of his coat, the man whispered to him, "Bologna, I want $100, and I want it quick."[90] Bologna tried to explain to him that he didn't have that much money, but the man replied, "I'll give you until next Monday evening. If I don't get it by that time you and your son will be blown into eternity."[91] Although there were dozens of policemen in the vicinity, watching a strike by New York butchers, Bologna's blackmailer wasn't bothered.

At about six o'clock in the evening, on August 15, Santi J. Polise, a tailor, hurried to the West Thirtieth Street Police Station in New York's Tenderloin district.[92] "I want a permit to carry a pistol," he excitedly told the sergeant on duty. "I'll fix 'em, the scoundrels!"[93] When asked why he wanted a pistol, he presented the police officer with a letter. As translated from the Italian, it read:

> *Be at One Hundred and Seventy-seventh Street and Third Avenue at 3 P.M. Aug. 16, and bring $200 with you. You are to walk down the elevated stairway and stand still when you reach the bottom. At 3 P.M. a man with a black mustache, wearing dark clothing, and with a white silk handkerchief around his neck, will pass you. As he does so he will touch you three times on the shoulder with his finger. He will then walk about five feet in front of you, turn suddenly and walk toward you. You are not to say a word, but just hand him the $200. Then go up the elevated steps, take the train, and be on your way.*
>
> *If you say a word to anyone about this letter or try to foil us we will kill you, your wife, and your child.*[94]

There was a black hand drawn at the bottom of the page with various mysterious signs. When Polise left the station, he said he would keep the appointment. A crowd numbering nearly five hundred collected at the appointed place and time to see what would happen. However, Polise was not one of them. Suddenly, another Italian felt a tap on the shoulder and a stranger barked, "Give me the $200."[95] A fight nearly ensued until the

In New York City, criminals congregated in one of the many stale beer dives. *Authors' collection.*

stranger—Billy Maynard, a pugilist—explained that it was all a joke. The disappointed crowd soon thinned out.

A day or two later, Max Sass, a dealer in trunks, received a letter. It read:

*Aug. 17, 1904*

*Mr. Sass: Kindly bring $500 for your life; bring the money at 7:30 P.M., Aug, 17, at One Hundred and Fifty-seventh Street and Third Avenue. Sure if not you will be killed and your five and the trunk store.*
*You sold me trunk for the Wiesebard murder you took from me a dollar.*[96]

It was signed with a drawing of a hand and the words "Don't forget!" Three years before, Sass had been suspected of selling the trunk in which a murdered man's body was found. However, he cooperated fully with the police, and it was subsequently determined that the trunk had been purchased in Virginia. When he received the letter, Sass did not believe it was a joke and took it to the police. He admitted he had been in constant fear of the Italians ever since the murder. Although there might not be agreement on what it was, everyone acknowledged that the Black Hand had arrived.

# 5
# WHAT'S IN A NAME?

*Sicily has suffered for centuries under a system of private ownership of property so onerous that life has become almost intolerable to the masses of the people, who, in spite of the wonderful fertility of the soil, are always on the verge of starvation.*[97]
—*Frank Marshall White*

By 1900, just over eleven thousand Italian immigrants had settled in Ohio. Twenty years later, there were more than five times as many. Although the police and the newspapers were on constant lookout for signs of a Mafia presence, it wasn't until the four Lonardo boys and the seven Porello brothers from Licata, Sicily, banded together in Cleveland in the 1920s that Ohio had a true Mafia family of its own.

"Known publicly as barbers, grocers, and restauranteurs, soon dominating the corn sugar trade," Frank Marshall White wrote, "the Lonardos and Porellos—allies on arrival, later deadly enemies—pursued covert sidelines in robbery, vice and Black Hand extortion."[98] Even then, much of the illicit activity in the state was controlled by Mafia families from Detroit and Pittsburgh.

In Columbus, the police were determined to prevent the Mafia from gaining a foothold. They were especially alarmed by the increasing occurrence of vendettas, although such blood feuds were not restricted to Italians. Many immigrant groups had brought the tradition with them.

What would be called the Finnelli (or Fannally) vendetta came to a deadly conclusion in Columbus on Sunday, April 24, 1904. By the following

Columbus Police Department patrol wagons in front of the West Broad Street station. *Authors' collection.*

Wednesday, eight suspects were in jail. Rumor was that the crime had been committed by a "secret murderous band."[99] Lorenzo Falcone (or Falconi), the sole witness to the shooting, claimed that a burglar entered the boardinghouse at Chase and Nineteenth Streets around midnight, brandishing a pistol. The intruder shot Michael Finnelli, who confronted him with a shotgun.

Because the residents of the boardinghouse were reluctant to notify authorities, the police didn't learn about the murder until seven hours later when David Reese, a railroad brakeman, reported that he saw a fully dressed body lying in the yard outside the building. Reese said he heard fifteen shots fired at 11:30 p.m., two of which sounded like a shotgun. It was not an uncommon occurrence on Sunday nights. The police suspected the dead man was embroiled in a vendetta with someone in the house and that the residents, who claimed they were all in bed at the time, were trying to protect the killer.

By the time the coroner examined the corpse, it had been taken inside, dressed in an undershirt and placed in bed by the helpful boarders. His "investigation strengthened the opinion that the man was shot while in the yard" and "that the shot came from above."[100] Many of those arrested told police that Falcone had a gun in his possession the day before the shooting, although he adamantly denied it. Frank Finnelli, a distant relative of the victim, said that two men pretending to be police officers had come to his house before the shooting, inquiring about an alleged robbery in the neighborhood.

On Wednesday morning, Detectives Victor Churches and Richard Owens went to a shanty on Twentieth and Chase Streets with Vincenzo Forgone. There, beneath a pile of rubbish, they found a .38-caliber revolver—Falcone later admitted he had purchased it from a pawnshop the previous week. After the shooting, he had given it to Forgone to hide for him. Despite strong suspicions that Falcone was the murderer, a case could not be built against him.

Then, on October 30, Churches received a visit from Pasquale Finnelli, who operated a boardinghouse at Twentieth Street and the Panhandle, and Nicolia Donato. Finnelli claimed that before Falcone left the country, he told his daughter Govina (or Giovina) Finnelli, "I have not peace in this country. I have to go to Italy for fear of going to the electric chair. I am guilty of murdering Michael Finnelli."[101]

The day before Finnelli was slain, Falcone had a heated argument with him over a keg of beer, and Finnelli slapped him—"a mortal insult among certain classes of Italians."[102] The beer had been purchased by a group of men, all of whom were required to chip in. They had an understanding that if anyone else came along and was treated to a glass of beer, the person who did the treating had to pay for the entire keg. Apparently, the father of Giuseppe Falcone had been given a beer and the others demanded that Lorenzo pay up. He refused.

Instead of striking Finnelli back, Falcone bided his time, waiting until all the other occupants of the house were asleep. He then persuaded his cousin Mattio Betruzzi to help him stage two robberies as a distraction. He would rob Finnelli's place while Betruzzi would rob that of Joseph Romana, a short distance down the street.

Just after midnight, Finnelli rose from his bed and walked out into the yard behind the house, presumably to visit the outhouse. Lying in wait, Falcone shot him dead, leaving the body where it fell. He also fired a double-barreled shotgun into the air to support the fake robbery scenario. Immediately afterward, Falcone re-entered the house, mingling with the other boarders, some of whom were wise to what had happened.

WHERE THE MURDER OCCURRED, A Dozen Italians Are Lodged in This Building.

A crude sketch of the house where Michael Finnelli mysteriously died. *Authors' collection.*

"Finnelli was in his night clothes when killed, but his body was afterwards dressed and the bullet holes in his breast covered with a clean white shirt in the hope that it might be made to appear that he had died from natural causes."[103] Some of the residents, Finnelli's widow among them, were interrogated at police headquarters and "sweated out singly and in pairs for several days."[104] However, they did not tell what they knew out of fear of retribution "by the local Maffia."[105]

Despite the suggestion that some sort of criminal organization was intimidating them, it was just as likely the Italians feared a family member would continue the vendetta and the police could not be able to protect them. Officer Churches later heard that Falcone was being held in Rosetta Valfortore, Province of Feggio, Italy, likely by relatives of Michael Finnelli.

Obviously, Finnelli and Fannally were different spellings of the same surname. Setting aside the fact that Italian names sounded strange to many reporters and police officers who struggled to pronounce, let alone spell them correctly, there were also cultural differences. For example, an item in the *Columbus Press-Post* on October 18, 1905, explained that there is a "peculiar practice in the southern part of Italy, where the wife retains her maiden name until the death of her parents, after which she takes her husband's name."[106] The criminals also used aliases to help obscure their criminal pasts, and most were illiterate. A prosecutor admitted that it was nearly impossible to obtain the correct names of any Italians involved in a crime.

Take the story of John Longo (or Long) and Antonio Pobolognono, two friends in Columbus. On December 2, 1906, Longo fired three shots at Pobolognono, then chased him with a stiletto. Pobolognono escaped to make a complaint to the police. The following August, Joseph (not John) Longo was dead, shot to death by Joe Pappano. Was it possible that Joe Pappano was Antonio Pobolognono?

According to Pappano, the shooting was the culmination of a vendetta born in Sicily fourteen years earlier when Joseph Longo and his relatives tried to kill him. As a result, Pappano fled to America and settled in Columbus. Eventually, Longo pursued him, and he was attacked at a house at 159 Vine Street. This time, Pappano pulled a gun and killed his assailant with two shots.

But in another account, Joseph Pappas (undoubtedly Pappano) was apprehended on July 27, 1907, by Officer Claude Leonard, who nabbed Pappas on the threshold of the boardinghouse he kept at 169 (not 159) Vine Street. Twelve hours earlier, Pappas had fled the scene with $200 and was believed to be on his way to Pittsburgh or Chicago. Although it was thought he had returned to the boardinghouse to obtain additional provisions to help him in his escape, he insisted he had been there the entire time.

Pappas readily admitted he had purchased a revolver after John (not Joseph) Longo teased him about the affections Pappas's wife had for him. He said his complaints to the police had been ignored. When he ordered Longo from his home, two nephews got drawn into the quarrel. Longo was bending over him, biting his head (his scalp did show lacerations), so he shot Longo to keep from being "chewed to death."[107]

Tried in September 1907, Pappas claimed he acted in self-defense. Charged with first-degree murder, he was convicted of manslaughter and sentenced by Judge Bigger to ten years in the Ohio Penitentiary. Pappano's wife appealed to the police, saying she feared she would be harmed by Longo's brothers, James and John—likely the same John Longo who attacked Pobolognono. Obviously, Pappas and Pappano were the same person and Pobolognono could have been, but probably wasn't.

The vendetta came to be viewed as yet another sign of Black Hand crime. And the Black Hand Society was seen as being a subset of the Mafia. The issue was where to draw the line. How large did a band of criminals have to be to constitute an organized crime entity? Certainly, the traditional Mafia and the individual Black Hand operations appeared to have much in common. As Black Hand literature was uncovered during various police raids, the following principles emerged:

- Obey the boss without question.
- Never reveal the organization's secrets.
- Always come to the aid of fellow gang members.
- Avoid entanglements with the law at all costs.
- Punish those who violate the rules.

Despite the best efforts of law enforcement to stamp them out, small bands of Italian criminals continued to gather together and worry their countrymen. Some of them developed rudimentary networks. Toward the end of October 1904, for example, Giuseppe "Joe" Lombardo was jailed in Wood County, Ohio, to await trial for murder. A police officer was sent from Columbus to act as interpreter and threatened by the Mafia. Although the officer was originally subpoenaed by the defense, he wound up acting for the prosecution. He took a statement from Joseph Cook, the foreman of an Italian gang camped at Walbridge, who told him that Lombardo had admitted to shooting Arthur Scott, age twenty. As a result, Cook was also threatened by agents of the Mafia.

The crime took place in the Italian quarter of Walbridge on Sunday evening, October 23, 1904. Scott and two friends had gone in search of three men who were said to have insulted a female friend of his. They subsequently became involved in a confrontation with Lombardo, who shot Scott twice in the heart. The Italian then fled. The Columbus police believed that Lombardo was the treasurer of the local branch of the Mafia, which was headquartered in Pittsburgh. At least five local Italians, also thought to be Mafia members, contributed money for Lombardo's defense.

The proprietor of a saloon at Chestnut Street in Columbus, Lombardo had "a bad reputation."[108] He also was employed with other Italians laying track for the Hocking Valley Railroad. Detective "Buck" Welsh of Toledo was brought in to apprehend Scott's killer. He rounded up three Italians who matched the description of the suspects and placed them in Sam Pecord's Saloon with a guard of twelve able-bodied men. But while he was away searching for three others, the guards permitted Lombardo to leave for a few minutes and he never returned. Two days later, he was captured on a train at Bucyrus as it was passing through town.

There had been rumblings earlier, but what really put the Black Hand on the map in Columbus was the murder of a Hungarian by an Italian at the north end of the St. Clair viaduct on October 15, 1904. This was an especially lawless region, just outside the boundaries of Columbus. James Peleno was suspected of killing Yohuko Gergersh and wounding Dobro Bordulo in front of the saloon of J.L. Roberts, 710 St. Clair Avenue. Officers Cheves, Churches and Harry James cornered Peleno in a shack on the old Columbus, Shawnee & Hocking Railroad property. The suspect purportedly admitted to having thrown away his revolver, although by the time he was booked at the police station, he denied all knowledge of the shooting or the gun.

Police Chief John F. O'Connor was an Irishman who struggled to deal with Italian crime. *Authors' collection.*

As near as the police could tell, there had been a group of Italians and an even larger group of Hungarians in the saloon. When one of the Italians lost some money in the sawdust on the floor, a fight started and moved outside. Stones, clubs and fists quickly began flying until a full-blown riot had erupted. While many people witnessed the slaying, nobody admitted to seeing it. An exasperated Police Chief John F. O'Connor said, "As long as they confine their shooting to themselves, I guess we will have to let them shoot and let the authorities of Milo look after them."[109] Again, the only thing that made it a Mafia or Black Hand crime was the fact that it had been committed by an Italian and that the witnesses wouldn't cooperate with the law.

A native of Ireland, Captain O'Connor was made chief under Mayor Robert H. Jeffrey following the sudden death of Chief John A. Russell in January 1904. He had served in the military for eight years and joined the police force in 1889, but he had no particular expertise when it came to Italian crime and not much interest in it. Although the department's Italian Unit did its best to solve the murder, five suspects were ultimately turned loose for lack of evidence. They had all been questioned by Coroner Joseph Murphy, but to no avail.[110]

On the Wednesday following the most recent murder, Chief O'Connor and James Dundon escorted Peleno to St. Francis Hospital in the hope that Bordulo, the Hungarian who had been wounded when Gergersh was killed, could identify him. However, Bordulo claimed to have been preoccupied watching a man play a slot machine when he was shot. Furthermore, he said he was too intoxicated to know who did it—this was despite the fact that the shooting took place outside the Roberts Saloon.

Bordulo had to be questioned via an interpreter, which cramped the officers' style when it came to interrogating him. He attributed the slaying of Gergersh to the Mafia or, as Chief of Detectives Dundon declared, "a branch of the Pittsburg Mafia...terrorizing the Italians of Columbus."[111] Sergeant Albanese and Officers Schiavo and Churches were warned that the group intended to "fix" them if they did not back off pursuing the murder investigation.

# 6

# YOUR CAT AND GOAT

*The crimes of Italy are peculiar; prompted by sudden passion, slighted love, jealousy, revenge for fancied insult, they are often in their circumstances terrible.*[112]
—*James Whiteside, M.P.*

Vincenzo Laposi of Old Forge, Pennsylvania, seemed to be well connected. When he was arrested on January 9, 1905, his pockets contained certain credentials "connecting the 'black hand' bands of Old Forge and Carbondale with 'the society of the Mafia' with headquarters at 42 Mott Street, New York."[113] These included a membership card granting him admission to all such organizations in the Lackawanna Valley. However, Laposi may have felt a little out of place at the Mott Street address since it was actually a longstanding Chinese mission.

Nevertheless, it was becoming increasingly difficult to deny that there was a criminal network of some sort, operating somewhere, involving somebody. But how great a threat was it? Not long afterward, in response to a rash of bombings in New York's Italian neighborhoods, Police Commissioner William McAdoo put Sergeant Petrosino in charge of a newly formed five-man squad of Italian-speaking detectives.

Born in Padula, Italy, Petrosino was a pioneer in the investigation of Italian crime in the United States. Although just five feet, three inches tall (Police Superintendent Theodore Roosevelt had waived the height requirement), he possessed courage in abundance. And he was motivated

The Pittsburgh public market, like similar operations, was based on the European model. *Library of Congress.*

by a desire to eradicate the Italian underworld because of the shame that it brought upon law-biding Italian Americans.

The Italian Unit had been Petrosino's idea. It was composed of Peter Dondero, George Silva, John Lagomarsini, Hugo Cassidy and Maurice Bonoil, the last being the only non-Italian in the group. Of French heritage, Bonoil spoke fluent Sicilian, and despite an Irish name, Cassidy (born Ugo Cassidi) was Italian, too.

After retired brigadier general Theodore A. Bingham took over as commissioner in January 1906, he expanded the size of Petrosino's squad from fewer than ten men to about thirty. He also organized another Italian squad in Brooklyn under Lieutenant Anthony Vachris, who had investigated the Catania murder. The same year, Pinkerton detective Dimaio formed an Italian unit of his own at the direction of William Pinkerton.

A year earlier, Dimaio, assistant superintendent of the Philadelphia branch of the Pinkerton Detective Agency, had roamed the Italian quarters of Chicago, Pittsburgh and other cities, dressed as a typical Italian laborer. His mission was to learn what he could of their criminal endeavors. The reports he produced led Petrosino to proclaim him the most knowledgeable man in America when it came to the Mafia.

Before the year was over, Dimaio was appointed head of the Pinkertons' Pittsburgh office. He believed that a unit of Italian agents could better investigate the increasing number of murders, kidnappings and extortions—the usual Black Hand stuff. Like Petrosino's agents, all of those he selected were either born in Italy or of immigrant parents. Very quickly, they found their services were in high demand as Black Hand crime spread throughout the country.

Shortly after noon on January 23, 1905, Gus Posteri (or Posturi), age twenty-four, was shot to death in Columbus, Ohio, by Tony Dangelo (or D'Angelo), age fifteen, his brother-in-law. The incident took place at the home of Joseph Dangelo on North Grant Avenue. Posteri, who married Joseph's daughter two years before, lived with his wife's family and worked in their fruit business. Apparently, Gus and his wife had become embroiled in an argument, and she called on her relatives for protection. He then pulled a gun and threatened to shoot his mother-in-law and sister-in-law. Later on, the trouble resumed, and Gus called the women "vile names."[114]

After some pots and pans were hurled, Anna, the sister-in-law, slipped out of the house and summoned Detectives William Rourke and Bernard Bergin. Even as they were looking into it, Tony entered the house, heard what Gus had called his mother and sister and, without warning, drew a revolver. Detective Rourke sprang at the young man but failed to secure the gun. Tony managed to fire one shot into Gus as he approached him.

The following month, Raffaello DeCisso (or DeCissi), who had recently arrived in Columbus from Virginia, was at a boardinghouse when Milio Pasquzzer, described as a tramp, struck him in the face. "I belong to the 'Black Hand' of New York and I have been sent here to kill you," Pasquzzer told DeCisso as he came at him with a knife.[115] Before DeCisso could draw his own stiletto, however, another Italian intervened. He later identified four other men—Frank Foueri, Frank and James Espasetti and James Carmille—as being members of the same gang.

The next day, Pasquzzer denied DeCisso's accusation in police court and was charged with vagrancy. It was openly wondered why DeCisso had fled the city, despite Officer Churches's assurance that he would be protected. Had the alleged gang members disposed of him? Although DeCisso was soon located, he disappeared once more. The police had little doubt he had been the victim of an extortion attempt and was frightened to the point of nervous prostration (as it was called then).

Legendary Detective William A. Pinkerton in his office. *Library of Congress.*

A little over a year later, on the afternoon of May 31, 1906, the fathers of Gus Posteri and Tony Dangelo—John Posteri and Joseph Dangelo—met on Naghten Street, drew their knives and began slashing at each other. "Dangelo received one cut from his nose back over his head to the base of the brain."[116] When the police arrived, he was attempting to staunch the bleeding with a sheet. During the fight, they were joined by their sons; Tony Posteri hurled a hatchet, and Charles Dangelo brandished a gun. At the city prison, Charles revealed that the two families had ambushed each other on a number of occasions since Gus was slain.

In July 1905, Salvadore Tonti of 179 Cypress Avenue, Columbus, received the following letter:

*You Millionaire:*

*You have more money than you need while we have none. Unless you meet me at Spring and Water streets on Saturday or Sunday nights at 8 o'clock* *and turn over $200 in cash we will blow your house up with dynamite and make sure that we kill you. Beware, we mean business.*

*MAFFIA*[117]

It might have been a joke, but Chief James Dundon was inclined to take it at face value. He assigned Detective E.M. Gordon, a Russian who knew five languages, and Sergeants Churches and Albanese to investigate. Tonti told them there were some "very bad Italians" in the city who met on a regular basis. Their leaders were from Patterson, New Jersey.

In August 1905, Bronx police were trying to track down the men who had been blackmailing a well-to-do merchant, Ignazio Calcaterra. Owner of four grocery stores, Calcaterra had been in the United States for fifteen years and had an estimated worth of $30,000. Another of the victims fled the country, but Calcaterra remained and was provided with armed guards day and night.

A generous and respected man in the community, Calcaterra received the following letter on August 16, 1905:

*Go to the end of Third avenue road. Walk round the big glass house three times with a lighted cigar in your hand. The first man that comes along give him the $2,000 cash, and your life will be saved. If you don't, we will kill you and your family, even your cat and goat and horse, and we will blow up your house. Don't tell this to anybody, but go and do it.*[118]

The letter was decorated with a heart and dagger, a tombstone bearing his name and a skeleton. It was signed "Black Hand Society." After showing the letter to the police, he was advised to do as instructed the following night. Two detectives were assigned to keep an eye on him, but nothing occurred. Two days later, he received a second, more terrifying letter, and the guard on his house was increased. Despite their vigilance, someone manage to chuck three bricks against his house, which signaled a third letter repeating the demands.

In his brief career, Petrosino had enjoyed great success in combatting Italian crime and had also made his share of enemies. However, no one risked killing him until he captured the chief of the Neapolitan Camorra. Ernico Alfano, known familiarly as "Erricone," had been giving the Italian police fits. Wanted for his involvement in a particularly gruesome murder, he was thought to have fled to New York. This was confirmed when Petrosino began receiving anonymous tips from New York's Neapolitan community. Erricone was so bold that he had hosted a large banquet for Camorra leaders at a Grand Street restaurant. Finally, Petrosino learned that Erricone was running a gambling den in a basement at 108 Mulberry Street.

Without letting his officers know who would be there, Petrosino sent four of them to raid the establishment. Erricone was among the men who were arrested. Sent back to Italy with an escort, Erricone let it be known even before he reached prison that the man who killed Petrosino would be richly rewarded.

In August 1905, a bomb was hurled at the home of Michael Palladina, a wealthy New York contractor, after he ignored four Black Hand letters demanding $2,000. "At the time Palladina, his wife and five children were asleep in the upper floor of the building, a brown-stone three-story and basement home."[119] None of the occupants was injured. The incident apparently evolved out of a dispute stemming from the celebration of the Feast of Our Lady of Mount Carmel involving competing factions.

At 5:30 on Thursday morning, February 15, 1906, three detectives entered a walk-in freezer at Pietro Miano's butcher shop in New York City, where they would remain for thirteen hours. Finally, at six o'clock that evening, Geocchino Napoli, age forty-five, entered the shop. Summoning the owner to the back of the store, Napoli informed him that he had come to collect the money he owed the "society." Miano gave him an envelope in which there were a number of one- and two-dollar bills, all of which had been marked by the detectives. After the man had departed, the detectives emerged from hiding and followed him to Bleecker Street, where they placed him under arrest for extortion.

For two months, Miano had been receiving letters demanding that he pay $700 to the writer "under penalty of having his shop and his family blown to pieces."[120] After discovering that other storekeepers in the neighborhood had been receiving similar threatening letters and that some had even paid, Miano went to the police. Sergeant Petrosino had remained outside the freezer while his men concealed themselves inside it. Although Napoli insisted he had nothing to do with the letters and could neither read nor write, he was found to have a quantity of wrapping paper in his room that matched some of the letters.

It was art imitating life when one month later, a one-reel drama, *The Black Hand*, was filmed and released by American Mutoscope and Biograph Company. Whether it was the first or simply the oldest surviving gangster-themed movie, *The Black Hand* claimed to be based on an actual incident that had recently taken place. The short film was practically a primer on how to commit a Black Hand crime.

On the complaint of Joe Lombardo, Joe Esposito and James Ross were arrested in an Italian saloon at 74 East Chestnut Street in Columbus early in November 1906. According to Lombardo, "They attacked him and beat him, threatening him that they would see that he was killed by the Mafia, of which they were representatives, unless he gave them a certain sum of money."[121] This may well have been the same Joe Lombardo who admitted killing Arthur Scott two years earlier.

Then on November 19, four Italians came to Columbus from Springfield. Sergeant Albanese and his men caught wind of their arrival and began searching for them in Locust Alley, where they were believed to be hiding. They suspected the men were planning to open a new headquarters for the local Mafia. Following the beating of Joe Lombardo at Frank Roberts's saloon, the Mafiosa, led by Dominic Jordan, had been driven out of Columbus. However, the quartet from Springfield were thought to have gone to Marble Cliff to meet with other members of their organization. Albanese was intent upon expelling them from the city before they had the opportunity to get established.

Victor Menzionetti of East Cherry Street, Columbus, began receiving threatening letters in November 1906. Then at two o'clock on the night of December 18, someone tried to gain admittance to the home of his father, C. Menzionetti, at 17 Blenkner Street. However, the senior Menzionetti went to the rear door of the dwelling and fired two shots, chasing the men off. He subsequently told Chief O'Connor that he believed he had been targeted by the Black Hand. Savanio Bandani was subsequently arrested by the police and charged with being the author of the threatening letters Victor received.

7

BEST DAY'S WORK

*Den patrolman arres' me and tell me him dead. I say I glad it is so;
I ready to sit in electrocution chair.*[122]
—*Charlie DeMar*

Giuseppe (aka Joseph) Giofritta's stay in Marion was an eventful one. Forty days after he set foot in town, he was arrested for the shotgun slaying of his forty-six-year-old brother, Louis. Indicted by a hastily convened special grand jury, he was quickly tried before a special petit jury.[123] But it was a half-hearted attempt at justice. The murder wasn't front-page news, even in Marion. The dead man was an Italian, after all, as was his alleged killer. The reporter couldn't even be bothered to keep the names straight or construct a coherent narrative. But this much is known: there were three Giofritta (or Guiffritta) brothers—Louis, Giovanni (aka John) and Joseph. Louis and John operated a fruit store (formerly a saloon) on North Main Street where Joseph joined them.

At about 4:30 a.m. on November 10, 1906, Louis Giofritta had rolled out of bed and gone downstairs to his general store at 235 North Main Street to fix breakfast. After a trip to the barn to tend to his horse, he returned to the store to eat his morning meal. When he was finished, he returned to the barn to prepare his horse and wagon to go to the market, where he operated a stand. Opening the large gate at the rear of the yard, he pulled the wagon out to the front of the store where his family would fill it with merchandise. At that moment, Louis was cut down by several loads of buckshot.

Collogero Vicarrio's apprehension was planned at the Bellefontaine police headquarters. *Authors' collection.*

Evidence suggested Louis's assailant was standing at the corner of the alley some thirty feet away. Surprisingly, none of his family members heard the gunshots. His body was discovered by his eldest daughter, Lena, age fourteen, when she went out to help him load the wagon. She immediately raced back to their apartments to raise the alarm. One of their neighbors, Edward Drake, stumbled across a couple of shell casings in a puddle. A small boy later found four loaded shells.

Although Louis's wife said she had no idea who would want to kill her husband, she was equally adamant that "no Americano did it."[124] The Giofritta family had been in the United States for about twenty-four years. Sicilians, they first settled in Indianapolis, then Dayton, before moving to Marion about 1902 and opening a general store. The father of five, Louis was regarded as a benefactor by many people due to his willingness to help them when they were having financial difficulties. However, a year earlier, he had been shot at by an unknown assailant who had called him out of the house.

When Joseph Giofritta came to Marion, he first asked to stay with Louis but was turned away. Louis was extremely jealous of any attentions paid to his wife, and Joseph was known to be quite fond of her. Consequently, Joseph moved in with his brother John. John and the Grassos were embroiled in an ongoing conflict with Louis over a debt they owed him.

Some two weeks before Louis's murder, a wagon belonging to John and the Grassos was burned and some items stolen.

A few minutes after five o'clock on the morning of November 10, 1906, Salvadore Hesso went with some of the other employees to the store's banana room. Joseph had not "come down to the cellar as he had been in the habit of doing."[125] Neither did he see Louis until after the shooting, which occurred about forty minutes later.

If there were witnesses to the slaying, there was no mention of them, but suspicion immediately fell on Joseph. While conducting his investigation, Chief of Police Levi Cornwell found a 16-gauge shotgun stashed in the store's cellar.[126] It was dirty and greasy, as though it had been recently fired, and was in a box that had been nailed shut and hidden beneath a pile of rubbish. In his testimony, Hesso stated that he had seen the weapon in Joseph's room just a few minutes before Louis was shot. He also recalled that the two of them had gone rabbit hunting with it several days earlier. Tano Grasso, identified by several people as the man who had been with Giuseppe when he bought the gun, confirmed it. So there was little doubt the shotgun was Joseph's. But that did not prove it was the murder weapon or that he had pulled the trigger.

About 100 Italians, as well as some "curious Americans" turned out for the funeral of Louis Giofritta.[127] More might have attended had not his murder, as well as those of two Italian railroad workers in the Erie yards, triggered a general exodus of Italians from Marion the day before. An estimated 125 employees of the Pennsylvania Railroad Freight Office, fearing for their lives, left town by train and interurban, headed in all directions. Their departure was facilitated by their employer.

After Charles Justice was appointed counsel for the defense, Evangeline Giofritta, John's daughter and "sweetheart" of Theodore Grasso (Tano's brother), was brought to the jail to serve as translator for her uncle and his attorney. She said Joseph had asked her to dispose of any of the shotgun shells that were still lying around the house. However, this bit of testimony was stricken as privileged communication. Evangeline was then prevailed upon to persuade Theodore to tell the truth, and he admitted he was with his uncle when he bought the gun.

One of the oddest facts to emerge during that trial was the claim of Frank Shaffer, a merchant's policeman who had been fired by the Giofrittas several days before the murder. He said Tano Grasso told him "that he need not watch their back door after that date."[128] To some, this was evidence that a conspiracy to kill Louis might have been in the works.

Sergeant Churches also testified, having served as the translator for the accused, many of the twenty witnesses and the Marion police. He had spent the night in the cell occupied by the suspects, hoping he would learn something about the murder, but they did not talk. Churches "explained that very few questions asked in English had been understood by the accused man."[129]

In the end, Joseph Giofritta was acquitted. No motive was offered, and the entire case rested on whether the shotgun was the murder weapon and, if so, whether Joseph had been the triggerman. He admitted he had purchased a 16-gauge shotgun but denied committing the murder. He said he had hidden the weapon precisely because he knew he would be a suspect. And none of the testimony established there was any trouble between the two brothers. Not wishing to push his luck any further, Joseph gathered up his belongings, said goodbye to his surviving brother and headed for Chicago on the last day of January 1907.

Louis Giofritta's murder would not be solved—not then, not ever. It would be overshadowed by other crimes within Marion's Italian settlement. In the week following Joseph's acquittal, the *Marion Daily Mirror* observed, "There is no question but that rather a weak effort is put forth by the officers to capture an assailant of an Italian, not the vigilance exercised that there would be if it were an American who was the victim. Americans apparently have little interest in the Italian."[130] The newspaper cautioned that if foreigners were allowed to escape punishment for their crimes, it would embolden them. However, the investigation had revealed that the Italian colony in Marion was split in half and that the two factions were quite jealous of each other. Local authorities worried that a branch of the Mafia had been organized there.

Fifty miles due south of Marion, the Columbus Police Department's three-man Italian Unit was working diligently to extinguish any outbreaks of Mafia-style activity in the capital city. In January 1907, Sergeant Peter Albanese waged an all-out war against Roberts's Saloon at 74 East Chestnut Street, forcing it to close. He had become convinced that it was the local headquarters of the Black Hand. One of the gang's members, Fred Deposita, ran off to Cincinnati, taking Mrs. Christina Vittori, the nineteen-year-old wife of Ralph Vittori, with him. Upon reaching Cincinnati, Christina adopted the name Grace Bernhardt. After an attempt was made on her life, she left town for a few days.

Having returned home, Christina/Grace heard a knock on the door. When she answered it, a man rushed in and slashed her face with a razor, inflicting a seven-inch gash on the left side and leaving her in critical condition. Word of the attack reached Christina's husband, Ralph Vittori, who traveled down to Cincinnati. He did not attempt to see his wife but informed police that he would have nothing further to do with her. However, he said her lover, Fred Deposita, had made an attempt on his life a year earlier. In response, the police jailed Fred on suspicion of attempting to murder Christina.

Despite the vigilance of men like Churches and Albanese, the Black Hand could not be extinguished. It had become a cottage industry, and every community of any size had Black Hand practitioners—or seemed to. In March,

Sergeant Victor P. Churches of the Columbus Police Department's Italian Unit. *Authors' collection.*

an unidentified Italian man was found hanging from a tree four miles outside of Canton, Ohio. Although he was initially thought to have committed suicide, the acting coroner noted that his skull had been fractured and his body badly bruised. Investigators began operating on the theory that he had been murdered by the Black Hand because that's where all investigations started in those days. And sometimes they turned out to be right.

While walking home early Sunday morning, March 24, 1907, "Joe" DeMar (aka Antonino Demma), age nineteen, was murdered in cold blood.[131] The cashier for Salvatore Cira & Company, DeMar lived on the outskirts of Bellefontaine, some forty miles west of Marion. He was accompanied by his cousin (possibly nephew) Charles "Charlie" DeMar and his uncle by marriage and employer, Salvatore Cira. All three were considered wealthy Italian businessmen. As they were passing along Troy Street, Joe was several paces ahead of the others.

The men were about one hundred yards away from Cira's home, where they all resided, when, without warning, two to six men purportedly fired at the trio from both sides of the street. Some of the shots "came from behind a barricade of corn fodder which had been set up during the night, and another shower of bullets [came] from a clump of brush."[132] Joe was struck by the first shot. Falling to the ground, he returned fire with his own pistol—three shots in the direction of his assailants—but was struck sevra' more times on the left side of his body. The nine bullet holes were so close together they could be covered by a silver dollar, suggesting he had been shot at close range—closer than eyewitness accounts indicated. However, it later proved to be buckshot.

Surprised by the ambush, seventeen-year-old Charlie and Salvatore claimed they had run for their lives. A safe distance away, Salvatore Cira pulled his own weapon and squeezed off six shots at the strangers, who made their escape through some vacant lots. He then ran home, ostensibly to obtain more ammunition. Charlie had no weapon and fled the scene in fright. A trail of blood confirmed that at least one of the assassins had been seriously wounded.

Salvatore suggested he was the intended target of the assassins. Three days earlier, he had received an anonymous letter demanding $1,000 or else. Furthermore, he claimed three suspicious Italians had been watching his store the night before. The newspapers reported that "the police [were] working on the theory that his wealth incited the 'Black Hand' to demand money, which Salvatore refused."[133] Aroused by the sound of gunfire, several local residents purportedly engaged the assailants in a running gun battle but gave up after half a mile. Both sides were believed to have sustained wounds.

Although he survived for two or three hours after the attack, Joe was unable (possibly unwilling) to provide a description of his assailants. He still had $200 in his possession, suggesting that robbery had not been the motive. Later that morning, the Bellefontaine police found two hats near the site of the shooting. Stiff and black, one had a stamp for a Columbus manufacturer and the other for a Canton one. In short order, Sam (likely Salvatore), a half brother, and Tony DeMar, a cousin, were arrested and charged with the murder of Joe. They were also partners in the firm of Salvatore Cira & Company. Both claimed to have been asleep at the time and were subsequently released.

Joe DeMar was one of six partners in the firm of Salvatore Cira & Company, which had been established in 1903.[134] Married to Provodeniza Amodes three years before, he "was planning to send money to Italy to his mother this summer to bring her to America."[135] Three years earlier, a teamster had collided with one of Cira's delivery wagons. An argument ensued, and the (unidentified) manager of the fruit store pulled a gun on the man and threatened to shoot him. The partners suggested Joe was murdered by Italians from another city who were jealous of their success and hoped to drive them out of business. In fact, Salvatore sent word to "Italian societies" in adjoining states, inquiring as to whether anyone was known to have been absent on the night of the crime.

At the inquest, Coroner Herbert was assisted by Sergeant Churches, who served as translator. Although Joe DeMar's murder was never solved, that wasn't the end of it. Roughly a year later, Salvatore Cira allegedly told Charlie DeMar that he had only ten days to live. He was mistaken. On April 9, 1908, Charlie turned tables on his boss and killed the forty-eight-year-old man. "Coroner Harbert found in Cira's pocket red-ink letters from Buffalo and Pittsburgh, written in Italian, but evidently threatening, because of some of the symbols drawn in them showing daggers plunged into a heart."[136]

Nathan Allen was in the vicinity of the Cira's fruit store when Cira was slain by his nephew. A cashier at the Independent Telephone Company of Bellefontaine, Allen lived with his family at Ohio Avenue and Oak Street. When he entered the fruit store to collect payment for the telephone, Charlie told him that "the old man" was on a rampage and that he should return in the afternoon. So Allen continued down the street.[137]

On his return, Allen saw that people were beginning to gather in front of the store. Pushing his way past them, he entered the store and saw Cira in a "half-sitting posture" in the rear of the building.[138] A pool of blood was forming on the floor around him. After he was arrested by Officer Polly, Charlie gave Allen the following statement:

*Me, a partner in fruit store with Salvatore, but he no pays me anyting; he say we make no money. He often says he kills me. I take bunch of de banana to grocery store and no gets receipt. Salvatore come in and give me devil. He say, "I killa you," and started for his room to get him gun. I pull revolver and shoot, one, two, tree, four time; den I run from him store and go down street. Den patrolman arres' me and tell me him dead. I say I glad it is so; I ready to sit in electrocution chair. I know dat I hits him until policeman tells me he dead. I tink he running after me wid gun. I not afraid to die now.*[139]

Police Chief Edward Faulder said that the murder of Salvatore Cira was the "best day's work ever done in Bellefontaine."[140] Cira had long been suspected of being the leader of the Black Hand. Mayor William Nevin also said the city in general was glad with the way things turned out. Most of the city's citizens felt it would be difficult to put together a jury who would convict Charlie DeMar of his murder.

Charlie told Chief Faulder that Salvatore had given Joe his overcoat to carry the morning he was murdered after instructing two confederates to shoot the man with the coat. As they were walking through an alley, a shot was fired and Joe dropped dead. When the two of them stopped running, Charlie claimed Salvatore stuck a gun to his head, threatening to kill him if he ever told anybody what he knew. According to the *Marion Daily Mirror*, Charlie said that prior to his shooting his uncle through the heart, "I prayed to God for months to give me strength to do this, and when the time came, He answered my prayer."[141]

Salvatore Cira's partners, Charlie included, agreed that Salvatore was promoting some Black Hand schemes of his own. He would travel frequently, remaining away for several days at a time. He claimed to be in Cleveland, but they suspected he was actually going to visit colleagues in the east. Salvatore always carried a shotgun with him. Feeling against the dead man was so strong in Bellefontaine that the local priest, Father Faurd, refused to hold a funeral service, say a mass over the body or permit him to be buried in the church cemetery because he was "not a good Catholic."[142] After three delays, the body was finally taken to potter's field and buried without ceremony.

Apparently, Salvatore Cira's widow, Mary D. Cira (daughter of Tony DeMar), did not hold any grudges. In 1910, the thirty-four-year-old woman was the head of a household that included three daughters (Mary, Perry and Josephine), three sons (John, Salvatore and Tony), her brother (Salvatore DeMar, age twenty-nine), father (Tony DeMar, fifty-three) and two boarders (Tony DeMar, twenty-six, and Charles Vicarrio, twenty-four). Collogero "Charles" Viccario would become a suspect in her husband's murder.[143]

# 8

# THE SIGNAL OF DEATH

*It is possible that for the public weal it would be preferable for John* [Joti]
*to continue his work as a Black Hand agent.*[144]
—Marion Daily Mirror

**F**ollowing his own conviction in a New York courtroom for kidnapping and extortion, Ignazio De Leonardo turned against his co-defendant, Pieto Pampinellia (or Paminnelli). A New York fruit dealer, Pampinellia and his wife had been charged with being the brains of the Black Hand operators. Taking the stand in his own defense on June 18, 1907, Pampinellia "placed his hands on his temples and brought them down slowly until they met at the throat."[145] Seeing this, De Leonardo refused to testify. When asked why, he replied, "Pampinellia has given me the signal of death. It's the black hand."[146] Ordered to take the stand, De Leonardo collapsed as soon as he laid eyes on the defendant.

Even without De Leonardo's testimony, Pampinellia was convicted of kidnapping seven-year-old Salvator Siatta from his Staten Island home the previous winter. The boy was eventually released, but his father denied paying the $10,000 ransom demanded, possibly fearing that such an admission would lead to his being further targeted. Like the American outlaw, the brigand was a romantic and often terrifying figure in Italian folklore who evaded capture by escaping from one papal state to another. A postal inspector said they had offered to return $2,000 to one victim, but the man refused to take it, insisting the money wasn't his. In another instance,

A fortune could be made at the produce market in Baltimore, Maryland. *Library of Congress.*

an Italian woman wouldn't surrender a threatening letter she had in her possession. "We finally had actually to tear her stocking off her leg before we got it," the inspector said. "She had it concealed there."[147]

Even in the United States, some Sicilian criminals maintained their traditional manner of dress, wearing the costume of the brigand in order to intimidate their countrymen. Salvatore Cira of Bellefontaine, for one, "dressed in a way to terrify the timid. It was he who used to wear the leather belt full of stilettos."[148] His intimidating appearance no doubt discouraged people from talking too freely. A crackdown on Italians carrying concealed weapons in New York resulted in over one hundred arrests, including seventy-five by Petrosino's Italian squad. According to a police report, "Ninety-five out of every one hundred Italians are armed with some sort of deadly weapon."[149]

Just the name—Black Hand—struck fear, often irrational, into the hearts of many Italians. Mrs. Dominica Friesticre, age nineteen, of Cleveland was charged with shooting Mrs. Concetta Mandillo with intent to kill. She was subsequently freed on June 8, 1907, however, after Mandillo defended her. She knew it wasn't personal; the young bride simply was caught up in Black Hand mania.

In his study of the Black Hand in Chicago, Robert M. Lombardo rejected as "myths" the idea that the Black Hand originated in Italy, that members of the Mafia and Camorra perpetrated Black Hand crimes in the United States and that only southern Italians and Sicilians were to blame.[150] For the most part, Lombardo claimed, Black Hand crime occurred in Chicago from 1907 to 1912. During this period, it was estimated that wealthy citizens received twenty-five letters a week from not only Sicilians and Italians but also Greeks, Germans (die Schwarze Hand), African Americans, opportunists, pranksters—anyone, really.

By Lombardo's count, 22 percent of the 267 victims were not Italian, nor were 17 percent of the offenders. Still, Italian-on-Italian crime was rife. The *Chicago Daily Tribune* reported that fully one-third of Chicago's Italian community was being extorted by the Black Hand. And in New York the situation was worse.

In June 1909, members of New York's Italian Unit were quoted as saying that for every extortion case reported, there were "probably two hundred and fifty of which nothing is said."[151] Of the 424 reported cases in 1908, only 33 were mentioned in the *New York Times*, *Il Progresso Italo-Ameircano* and *L'Araldo Italiano*. If each of the reported cases represents 250 unreported ones, then the actual number for 1908 was more than 100,000. Arthur Woods, deputy police commissioner of New York City, insisted that "it has been found in almost every case that a man arrested for a Black Hand crime has been convicted of a crime in Italy."[152]

Historian Humbert Nelli claimed that none of the "141 Black Hand cases that took place during 1908 in New York, Boston, Philadelphia, Baltimore, Chicago, Pittsburgh, Cleveland, New Orleans, Kansas City, and San Francisco" occurred outside of an immigrant district.[153] In other words, Italians who left the colonies were seldom if ever victims of Black Hand crime.

Columbus was not as sectioned off as many cities. The Italians, Greeks, Hungarians, Bulgarians, Macedonians and other immigrant groups lived in proximity, if not harmony. This was evident when Werner Stefo was found early Sunday morning, June 23, 1907, in a field near Church Street and St. Clair Avenue, with two bullet holes in his head. He was believed to have been killed Saturday night, not far from the Columbus, Shawnee & Hocking Railway tracks by the village of Grogan. Both bullets passed completely through his head, one from cheek to cheek and the other entering about two inches higher and exiting from the base of the brain, severing the spinal cord. Robbery clearly wasn't the motive, because he had $171.50 and a

Immigrants were hired to pick berries on farms outside Baltimore. *Library of Congress.*

watch and chain on his body. He was not identified until someone was found who could translate the Macedonian letters found in his pockets.

The letters revealed that Stefo was probably the victim of a vendetta that had originated in his home country. Two years earlier, he had come to the United States to escape his tormentors. He first went to the home of two of his sons in Terre Haute, Indiana. However, one day he recognized his enemy on the street, so he fled to Monetta, near Bucyrus, Ohio, to stay with a brother. Finally, he came to Palestine, a settlement not far from where he was murdered. He had secured work at a Cleveland, Akron & Columbus Railroad construction camp on Saturday. The tower watchman had spotted him walking along the track late that evening with another man. It was speculated that he was lured to the place where the murder occurred.

Detectives William G. "Shelly" Shellenbarger and Bernard Bergin, the latter on the verge of retirement, worked the Stefo murder case. At his funeral, they gathered information on three suspects: Dano Petri, twenty-two; Nick Trico, twenty; and Demetri Christo, age unknown. The men, all either Macedonians or Bulgarians, were the only ones who knew Stefo was arriving in Columbus. Petri, Stefo's cousin, had received a letter alleging Stefo would have $500 on him.

The three men lived together in a shack by the Pan Handle Railroad shops. Interviewed by two separate interpreters, they all had differing stories about when they got home on Saturday night. One said they were home all evening; the second that they were home by ten o'clock; and the third that they didn't arrive home until three o'clock in the morning. Their Greek neighbors agreed it was closer to 3:00 a.m. When the suspects were later searched at the police station, Petri was found to have $178.77 in his possession and Trico $94.74. Christo was picked up with a dagger, three revolvers and three boxes of cartridges. One of the pistols was a .38, the same caliber used in the murder. It had been fired recently and had two empty chambers. However, they all continued to deny any involvement in the murder.

Giuseppe "Joseph" Di Giorgio was known as the "Banana King of Baltimore." A native of Sicily, he had come to the United States in 1888 at the age of fourteen. After working a few years as a fruit jobber, he settled in Baltimore, where he soon established himself as a middleman. In less than ten years after his arrival in Baltimore, Di Giorgio was president of four fruit companies, through which he controlled "the importation and sales in the Baltimore areas of fruit from California and Italy, and of bananas from Central America."[154] Along the way, he had dethroned Antonio Lanasa, head of the Lanasa-Goffe Steamship & Importing Company, who was now deep in debt. Lanasa set about bringing down Di Giorgio by hiring a Black Hand gang to go after him—echoes of the Matranga-Provenzano feud seventeen years earlier in New Orleans.

For a brief time, Di Giorgio, Lanasa and Antonio Constantine Goffe had been partners in the Atlantic Fruit Company. However, Di Giorio doubled-crossed them, making a side deal with the United Fruit Company of Boston and squeezing them out. Lanasa and Goffe went on to found their own shipping business. Di Giorgio subsequently received a letter that could have been mistaken for a solicitation from a charity. It read, "You have become prosperous. You owe something to your countrymen. We want you to make a contribution to the Patriots."[155] However, it was signed "Mano Nera."

A week later, another came: "You have not answered us. We want ten thousand dollars. If we do not get it you and your family will have trouble—Mano Nera."[156] This time, Di Giorgio did not ignore it but passed it onto the police before making a business trip to Cuba. While he was away, a bomb exploded on December 10, 1907, in his handsome home in the Baltimore suburb of Walbrook. Although the porch was destroyed and the windows and doors shattered by the blast, Di Giorgio's family escaped injury. Immediately, a police guard was posted, not only at his home but also at those of five other wealthy Italians. And they were given orders to shoot at any suspicious characters they encountered. Salvatore Lupo was subsequently arrested in Buffalo, New York, and charged with complicity.

The case against Lanasa was built upon the testimony of his co-defendants, Lupo and Joseph Tamburo. While visiting Pittsburgh to arrange for Di Giorgio to receive extortion letters, Lupo and a man named Phillipo (or Filipo) Rei (or Rea) had a conversation with Lanasa in which Lanasa said, "If we kill Joseph Di Georgio [*sic*] I will be the banana king of Baltimore."[157] At the same time, Lanasa hired Lupo to bomb Di Giorgio's house. Lupo testified that he left Pittsburgh, intending to arrive in Baltimore on December 10, but was delayed. As a result, the house had already been dynamited by the time he reached Baltimore, making him an accessory to attempted murder.

Chief of Detectives A.J. Pumphrey of Baltimore, accompanied by seven of his men, tried to extradite twenty-two-year-old John Scalatta (aka Scarlatta or Schlatta), who was wanted on a charge of dynamiting Di Giorgio's house. The detectives believed Black Hand men were conducting the wholesale manufacture of explosives in Cleveland and "that several hundred dangerous Italians" had found asylum in the city.[158]

In a hearing that lasted ten days, Scalatta fought being extradited to Maryland. Despite the testimony of fifty Italians who swore Scalatta was in Cleveland at the time, Judge Phillips ruled on January 16 that Scallata must return to Baltimore to stand trial.[159] Ultimately, Lanasa was found guilty and sentenced to ten years in prison and Lupo to fifteen months. But Scalatta, the remaining bomber, forfeited bail, and his ultimate fate is unknown.

Another wealthy Baltimore Italian (and resident of Walbrook), Dominick Miccio, received several letters, although the handwriting does not match any of the others. It was written in crude English:

*Mr. Dominick Miccio—With this letter I let you know that you have taken very little account of me. That will do. Look out, now, for you carry a very bad verdict on your shoulders. This verdict is to disturb all your business and to destroy your life, even though you build a house of iron, because I, Constantino Anarche, with but a single word, can destroy anything I want. I have under my command three hundred and sixty thousand persons. Sour, and very sour for the one who falls in our hands, Mr. D. Miccio. We have just the same right to live on you people who have large business. I, Constantino Anarche, will compel you, before five days, to make up a flower which will not disturb anything: this flower you will make it of six hundred dollars, which you will do it secretly without letting anyone know it, otherwise it will be worse for you. In doing this I will take an oath under our blood and oaths that all your bad sentence that you carry will end. You can navigate easily with your business. This flower that you do send by registered letter, and when we send to get it we will send a poor innocent person; be careful and do not say anything to the law, and what you do, do it with a good heart, and secretly I will promise you that all your troubles will be ended, and you may walk night and day without fear. Send letter to A. Constantino Anarche, Pinehill, Pa.*[160]

The Di Giorgio bombing foreshadowed events that would unfold in Columbus three years later. But there may have already been a connection to Black Hand activity in Columbus. "Regarding [Joseph] Catalona," the *New York Tribune* reported, "Joseph Serio, a saloonkeeper, testified that his brother in Columbus, Ohio, informed him by telephone that he had been receiving Black Hand letters from Baltimore threatening him with death if he did not comply with the demands of the organization."[161] Catalona offered to intercede on the brother's behalf but said he would have to clear it with the "head one" in Brooklyn. Seven days later, Catalona read him a message indicating that his brother would not be bothered any further. Presumably, Joseph Serio's brother in Columbus was Frank Serio.

When a beat officer became curious about activity in an Italian restaurant at 37 Clay Avenue in Pittsburgh's Little Italy, the chief dispatched two Italian-speaking officers—Peter Angelo and Charles Aymer—to investigate. Working undercover, they found that the "kitchen" was equipped with a forge and the "white-aproned chef" was engaged in making stilettos. He also kept an assortment of revolvers and other weapons. Consequently, on Christmas Eve 1907, a police detail composed of detectives from ten cities—some fifty in all—overpowered the operator of the restaurant and forced their way in.

Beneath a table in the kitchen was a trapdoor leading down a flight of stairs into the cellar. An underground escape passage branched off of it and opened onto an alley adjoining Clay Alley. When they burst in, they surprised seventeen young men stripped to the waist and holding stilettos. They were being taught by two older men how to attack a dummy with knives. Scrawled on the walls of the cellar were the words "Camaristi; Mano Nora [*sic*]," along with "weird drawings of assassinations, bleeding hearts with daggers through them."[162] This school for assassins was being

Two to four families of berry pickers occupied each two-room shanty. *Library of Congress.*

conducted by Vincenzo Toya and Antonio Nicola, who had been pegged by the New York police as leaders of the Black Hand.

After an intense struggle, all nineteen men were carted off to jail, and some five hundred weapons were confiscated. "The police admitted that Pittsburgh [was] the headquarters for a number of the worst groups of Black Hand in the country, and that members are instructed [there] to do work in other cities."[163] They estimated some four hundred members of the Black Hand were in Pittsburgh alone. Reporters mentioned that the raid was somehow connected with the killing of Phillipo Rei and also that some helpful information had been provided by Captain A.J. Pumphrey of the Baltimore police, who was in town searching for evidence related to the Di Giorgio case.

On Sunday evening, July 7, 1907, there was an attempted shooting at Number 2 Empire mine near Bellaire, Ohio. It occurred in the Italian quarter. Two Italians, who refused to identify themselves out of fearing of being killed, were locked up while the police were searching for a third on a charge of shooting with intent to kill. The police suspected that the Black Hand Society was involved.

A man had entered a company-owned house on Sunday evening and demanded money. Because they did not have any, the man, whom they did not know, tried to shoot the mother and the father, firing four or five shots. However, their twenty-year-old son deflected his aim. The young man then ran to get the police, and three officers were dispatched to investigate. "Going back on the street car the young man who informed was attacked by two strange Italians who tried to choke him, almost tearing his shirt off."[164] The conductor intervened, and one of the men was arrested. Instead of continuing home, the frightened victim went to the police station and asked to be locked up. Also locked up was another man who had threatened to kill the young man's father if he told the police anything.

Although dozens of Italians had witnessed the shooting, none of them claimed to know who he was or would provide a description. Two days later, about 30 "tough looking Italians" came to the city building, attempting to gain entrance to the hearing. Mayor Wassman cleared the courtroom of everyone except the father and son. Police believed that 150 Black Hand members proliferated in Bellaire, most of whom had been involved in the riots and murders at Scranton, Pennsylvania, several years earlier.

The young man claimed that he was threatened with physical harm if he did not pay twenty dollars to join the society. He now believed he would have to leave Bellaire or they would stab him to death. Many of the crimes committed around Bellaire, he said, were the work of the Black Hand, but they always used someone from out of town to carry it out and covered his tracks so the police could not track him.

Despite what had taken place in Ohio, Pennsylvania and elsewhere, Lieutenant Petrosino in New York asserted just after Christmas, "There is no national, or even local, head of the Black Hand society that had control over the hundreds of little bands which ply their trade of blackmail. If there was any head, it would be right here in New York."[165] He could detect no evidence of a central organization among the more than two thousand Black Handers he had arrested in the past year. The fact that they used similar methods was due to imitation rather than training, down to copying the exact wording and symbols and their threatening letters.

Petrosino had long advocated that the U.S. government work with that of Italy to vet immigrants to ensure the criminals were not admitted. Over the course of his career, he was credited with returning some five hundred Italians to Italy to face prison sentences for crimes they had committed before coming to the United States. Not surprisingly, he became a marked man.

# 9

# THE GREAT BUGABOO

*Foreign criminality is actually more of a scare than a fact.*
*It is a great bugaboo, the same as the Black Hand.*[166]
—*Francis J. Oppenheimer*

rancis Oppenheimer wore his politics on his sleeve. His article "The Truth about the Black Hand" was published by the National Liberal Immigration League, which opposed all measures to restrict immigration. Although Oppenheimer no doubt wanted to believe that foreign criminality was "more of a scare than a fact," those who were closer to it—the immigrants themselves—knew better.[167] After all, they were by and large its victims.

According to one study, just over 90 percent of the foreign-born male offenders committed to New York prisons in 1904 spoke English. The "criminal class [had] but little trouble to pick up the language," presumably because it aided them in performing their criminal endeavors.[168] Their victims, on the other hand, were far less likely to speak English, increasing their isolation and their reticence when it came to seeking help from the police.

Although it was unlikely that many so-called Black Hand crimes were connected, nobody could say for certain. But most people tended to believe in conspiracies, including eighteen detectives from Baltimore, Harrisburg, Syracuse, Pittsburgh, New York and Wheeling. The *Urbana Daily Courier* echoed their declaration on January 9, 1908: "Black Hand in Cleveland. Ohio City Said to Be Center of Organization's Operations."[169]

A typical banana vendor peddles his wares on the streets of New York City. *Library of Congress.*

However, one fact that could not be denied was that many so-called Black Hand letters were fakes. What is believed to have been the first "fake" Black Hand letter in Chicago appeared in 1904. Dubbed the Nicoletti affair, it was "merely a case of a Greek citizen writing himself a Black Hand letter, posing as a man in great fear, getting himself sworn in as a special policeman and going out with his police powers and taking a good fall out of another Greek citizen who had displeased him."[170]

Anyone with a pen, paper and the price of a stamp could produce a Black Hand letter. The challenge for law enforcement was recognizing the real ones. There were no established criteria for distinguishing real Black Hand letters from phony ones. Age, ethnicity and national boundaries were not barriers to would-be Black Hand letter writers. And their motives were just as varied.

For example, during several weeks in November 1908, a dozen or so female residents of East Hanover Street in Hamilton, Ohio, had been receiving letters threatening their homes and lives if they did not leave the neighborhood at once. "Their characters were defamed in the vilest manner and the writer threatened to blind their children with caustic."[171] A police investigation implicated a Mrs. Nellie Grabel, who was charged with being the author of at least some of the letters. However, her hearing was postponed when the prosecution witness, Mrs. Martin Schallip, found a letter on her porch warning her to drop the charges against Mrs. Grabel or she would be killed and her home dynamited. In response, a cordon of heavily armed police was assigned to patrol East Hanover Street in hope of preventing any attempt by the Black Hand Society to dynamite homes.

On February 8, 1909, Mrs. Grabel was granted her liberty after the charge against her was reduced to criminal libel. Her counsel successfully argued, "The letters were unspeakably vile, but the expressions were all couched in slang."[172] He convinced Judge Warren Gard that the language was meaningless and, therefore, not libelous. Clearly, Black Hand was a game anyone could play, leading Lieutenant Joe Petrosino of the New York Police Department to conclude: "As far as they can be traced, threatening letters are generally a hoax"—but not always.[173]

Once targeted by extortionists, many victims found that the blackmailers could be unrelenting, as Ignata "Joseph" Colluccio learned the hard way, assuming he learned at all.[174] In June 1907, Colluccio, who worked as a sweeper (alternately a railroad section hand) at Union Station in Columbus, was cornered by a handful of Italians who "told him he either had to pay tribute or they would administer a beating."[175] Although he didn't want a beating, he didn't want to give up his money, either, so he refused. The following evening, he was walking along Naghten Street when he ran into them again. They made him the same offer, and once again, he turned them down. This time they did deliver a sound thrashing.

Convinced he was dealing with the Mafia, Colluccio turned to a man named John Bove for help. Bove told him he would need thirty dollars to "deposit at the police station to secure their arrest."[176] After taking the money, however, Bove disappeared. Eight months later, on the morning of February 4, 1908, Officer Louis Spohn was making his rounds near Third and Naghten Streets in Columbus, Ohio, when he noticed a handful of Italian men examining a letter.[177] Curious, he stopped to question them. He learned that it had been left in Marsino's Saloon and was addressed to Colluccio. Spohn returned to police headquarters, where he had the letter translated by Sergeant Victor P. Churches. It was dated Columbus, Ohio, February 3, 1908, and read:

*Mr. Collucio* [sic]—*We have written you a letter before this one, and you have not brought the $100. Tomorrow evening, February 4, at 7:30 p.m. near the steps of the old post office, a pretty woman will give you the password, "Godfather," and you give the money. Do not advise the police and bring the money, otherwise you will be killed. Signed, Black Hand.*[178]

Colluccio was frantic. He did not have access to $100 in cash and believed he would be killed if he did not pay up. The police assured him they would try to locate the letter writer. In September 1908, Colluccio again made the news. For the third time in two years, he got mugged, this time losing $99 and a gold watch. The incident occurred on Naghten Street near High Street (he lived at 115 East Naghten). The year before, Colluccio was assaulted in the same neighborhood and relieved of $30. He had the reputation for "showing his roll" when he was under the influence of alcohol.[179] Four months after that, he was robbed of $210. This time, he recognized one of the robbers as one of his countrymen. So Colluccio, with the assistance of an Italian lawyer, managed to get $150 back by promising not to divulge the robber's identity.

Joe Colluccio worked sweeping up at Union Station in Columbus. *Authors' collection.*

A few days before the latest incident, it became widely known that Colluccio was carrying nearly one hundred dollars, and he was advised by Stationmaster McCabe and Officer John Lee to deposit it for safekeeping. However, he declined. Following the most recent assault, Colluccio turned up at the city prison with two deep gashes on his head, a cut on his left jaw and a bruise on his left leg. His head and shoulders were covered with bruises, and his face was a mass of blood. He knew one of the men and provided police with a good description.

Many Black Hand bands sought to recruit new members from the ranks of their victims. On February 4, 1908, six Italian men were arrested in Canton, Ohio, for threatening the life of Mike Altire because he would not join their gang. Chief of Police Smith and Detectives Ryan and Brisbin subsequently discovered that the same men made similar threats against Louis Santis and Mr. Bell, partners in a local saloon. They demanded that the saloonkeepers pay them tribute to join their group or the gang would dynamite the new brick building they occupied. Although it was claimed that Felix Rich had also been threatened, he denied it.

Detective Ryan and Officer Penley went to the home of Joseph Santangelo on a report that the gang had met there. "In a room there the officers found several letters written in Italian coming from Niles, South Bend and a small town in Pennsylvania, a revolver that was out of commission and a razor."[180] Penley intended to give them to some "trustworthy" person to translate. "There may be a little trouble in fastening the guilt on the right parties," said Chief Smith, "but we will do all we can to kill the local organization in its infancy."[181]

Four days later, the men went on trial in Mayor Trumbull's court, and Sam Dominic, the alleged leader of the gang, was bound over to the grand jury. James Phillipo testified "that he had been sent to Altire with demands by Dominic and a man named Joe, who had escaped from the officers when the arrest was made."[182] Phillipo was told on several occasions to ask Altire for the money and kill him if he refused. Although Dominic denied everything, one of the Altire daughters stated that she heard him say "I'll fix your father" when she encountered him prior to the arrests.[183]

Under the headline "Money or Life," the *Columbus Press-Post* ran an exposé of Black Hand activities in Columbus. D'Angelo, a resident of North Grant Avenue near Naghten Street, purportedly had received a number of Black Hand letters.[184] (This is the Joseph Dangelo who was involved in an earlier vendetta.) He was believed to be worth $15,000. But

Charles Amicon's Bryden Road residence is seen in the foreground. *Columbus Metropolitan Library.*

when Detective Ollie Hamer investigated the matter, D'Angelo, described as a wealthy "huckster," initially denied there was any truth in it. The first letter, which he ignored, was said to have demanded he pay $5,000 in tribute. However, when other letters followed, threatening dynamite bombs, he sought help from the local authorities. Everyone who was threatened was reluctant to talk about it. D'Angelo found a bomb at his door with a warning that the next one would be live.

Rumor had it that there were no more than five or six Black Hand conspirators in Columbus and that they met not far from the Amicon Brothers' commission house on Naghten Street. According to the article, the suspects "live in a certain degree of luxury that has attracted attention to them from the fact that they have no other known resources, never being seen in any legitimate employment, always dressing well and living, as it were, at the top of the heap."[185] The Black Hand letters are dropped into mailboxes "here and there with but slight chances of detection."[186]

Frank Serio of 150 East Town Street, who had been in Columbus less than eighteen months, told a *Columbus Press-Post* reporter that the Black Hand was a terror to his people but he had not been molested since his arrival in the city. He lied. An anonymous source told the reporter that Serio had already paid some $30,000 in protection money and that nearly every wealthy Italian in the city had either been threatened or had paid off the extortionists.[187] (This may well have been the brother of Joseph Serio on whose behalf Joseph Catalona had intervened with the "head one" in New York.) Agostino "Gus" Iannarino (D'Angelo's neighbor), who lived on Grant Avenue just north of Spring Street, admitted he had received several Black Hand letters (his house would later be dynamited). Frank Macusia, who had a stand in Central Market, paid $500 in tribute, then another $500 when he talked too much. Frank Lascola, a fruit vendor in in the market, paid $200.

The only non-Italian in Columbus receiving Black Hand letters was William M. Fisher, whose son procured an automatic revolver. After that, any suspicious-looking Italians who entered their produce store found themselves staring down a gun barrel. A few of them assured him that the letter mailed to his father had been a mistake. However, when two of them gave him a hard time, he chased them into the alley "with bullets barking around their heels."[188] Fisher was the maternal grandfather of author James Thurber, who wrote about his memories of roaming through his grandfather's fruit and vegetable company, William M. Fisher & Sons.

The use of dynamite bombs put the community on edge. On Saturday afternoon, April 4, 1908, "two mysterious grips" were left sitting by a telephone pole at Broad and High Streets in Columbus, from 1:00 to 6:00 p.m.[189] Not one of the "tens of thousands" of people who passed by them paused to investigate the "mysterious packages." A writer for the *Columbus Press-Post* wrote, "In these days of explosives, dynamite bombs, and Black Hand Terrors, people are not impulsive in gathering up hand bags, grips, satchels and suit cases that may be lying about without apparent owners."[190] Finally, Officer Mack Murray summoned a police wagon to haul the packages to city prison for inspection.

The same month, a suspicious-looking man was about to place a package in the window grating of a Pittsburgh hotel when a bulldog seized his leg and wouldn't let go. The people who came to the man's rescue discovered that his package contained a bomb that could have wrecked the entire hotel, which held about 150 people at the time. In Cleveland, Black Handers threatened to blow up the home of Salvatore La Mandia in Cleveland and to kill him and his family. A letter demanded that he give them $1,000 at once. And when several prominent citizens in the village of Minerva received Black Hand letters demanding money, a "Canton police officer, called in to help unravel the mystery of threats, waited all night near a hole in the village sidewalk where Harry Couch, banker, had left a box of waste papers as a substitute for the $500 he had been ordered to deposit as the price of his life."[191]

T.S. Elliot said, "April is the cruellest month," but the ones to come were even worse.

# THE WHITE HAND SOCIETY

*[T]here must be developed a uniformed corps of police,*
*made up of men—south Italians—as brave and as reckless and as honest*
*as were Wild Bill Hickok and Seth Bullock and Colonel Sanders and*
*Bat Masterson and the others who terrorized the road-agents*
*and cattle-thieves of our own wild West forty years ago.*[192]
*—Lindsay Denison*

There were various proposals from all quarters for tackling the Black Hand problem. One floated by author Lindsay Denison in *Everybody's Magazine* called for assembling a sort of super posse composed of men on the order of such legendary gunfighters such as Bat Masterson and Wild Bill Hickok. In addition to knowing "the secret language of the Italian secret societies," Denison specified that the "members of this police corps must be no respecters of tradition or of persons in authority."[193] He did not explain what he meant by this, except to suggest that law enforcement would sometimes shield criminals from prosecution.[194] But he wasn't the only one who had noticed.

However, Joseph Petrosino, head of the New York Police Department's Italian squad, didn't believe that greater force was the answer. In his opinion, it was "ignorance of the blessings he might enjoy in this country that [was] holding back the Italian-American citizen."[195] Petrosino argued that they needed "a missionary more than a detective" to go among the immigrants and impart knowledge of America's history, the functioning of

Lindsay Denison believed a Bat Masterson was needed to combat the Black Hand. *Library of Congress.*

the government and their constitutional rights. "If the Italian coming to this country only knew that the American had secured his independence by as great a struggle [as they had in their own country], there would be an immediate bond of sentiment of the purest kind between him and his new brother-citizen."[196] Before the Black Hand menace was finally eliminated, both approaches would be tried. Still, there always seemed to be a little more money for guns than education.

With the tacit support of the 1,400 members of the Unione Siciliana, 800 members of the Societe Trinacria and 250 members of the Italian Chamber of Commerce, the White Hand Society of Chicago was organized in September 1907. Its headquarters was in the Masonic Temple Building, in front of the Italian Consul. "Stirred by the recent kidnapping of Giuseppe Giunta, whose father Antonio Giunta, received several threatening letters demanding $500, the White Hand Society adopted resolutions demanding increased police protection for Italian residents of Chicago."[197] They promptly pledged $10,000 to combat the blackmailers.

This was remarkable on several counts. Immigrant communities typically prefer to ignore the existence of a criminal element within their own midst or denounce such accusations as an ethnic slur. To their credit, the White Hand Society both acknowledged it and set about addressing it. What is more, Italy's Foreign Minister Thomas Tittoni gave it his official approval, and plans were made to take the society international. Branches would soon spring up in other U.S. cities.

The White Hand Society also questioned whether Chicago's largely Irish police force was equipped to deal with Italian or Sicilian criminals. Not only were the officers unable to understand the language and the customs of the "foreigners," but they exhibited little interest or enthusiasm in investigating related crimes. And so the immigrants were left to police themselves.

During the seven weeks following the society's formation, ten blackmailers had purportedly been driven out of Chicago through its efforts. But the membership of the White Hand felt a need to hire their own "official Sherlock Holmes" to carry out its mission—Godfrey Trivisonno.[198] He arrived in Chicago from Pittsburgh on January 2, 1908, having previously seen service as a detective in the office of the Italian secretary of state at Rome, Italy. He was installed as the secretary of the White Hand Society and, according to *La Tribuan Italiana*, would "receive secretly all communications

In Hollywood's version, Gene Kelly, as Johnny Columbo, fought the Black Hand. *Authors' collection.*

90

your countrymen desire to give the organization and who in turn will take immediate steps to give full satisfaction and protection."[199]

Dr. Camillo Volini, one of the leaders of the White Hand, proclaimed, "We feel we have them on the run, but we also realize perpetual vigilance will have to be the price of our redemption, from the exactions of these bands of criminals."[200] He described Trivisonno as the "war secretary" of their group. Among his duties was to educate respectable Italians on how to discover Black Hand passwords, how to keep secret the fact that one identified a Black Hand member and how to inform the White Hand without endangering oneself and one's family.

One of the White Hand Society's most important contributions was a serious study of Black Hand crime, published in September 1908 (in English and Italian), titled *Studies, Action and Results*. It consisted of six conclusions:

*1. The Black Hand was a signature or method of extortion that often involved the use of threatening letters.*

*2. The Black Hand was not a vast criminal organization; small groups of independent criminals committed Black Hand crime, and some of these groups were composed of offenders who had left Italy to escape the Italian police.*

*3. Black Hand crime occurred only in communities that exhibited certain social conditions.*

*4. Black Hand letters escalated in their threats in order to intimidate the victim, and someone known to the victim, a "friend," was often involved in the extortion scheme. Additionally, Black Hand criminals used acts of violence such as breaking a window, firing a revolver in the dark, or placing a small bomb under a stairway to demonstrate the seriousness of the threat.*

*5. Black Hand crime had a detrimental effect on the Italian community. Not only had it led to widespread fear, which kindled feelings of hatred and vengeance, it also led to a profound distrust of the American government because of the failure to control it.*

*6. The White Hand Society argued that the press's unfair portrayal of Black Hand crime caused native [born] Americans to discriminate against Italian immigrants.[201]*

Unfortunately, by focusing more attention on Italian lawbreakers, the White Hand Society provoked a backlash against the Italian community as a whole. By the time the movement ran out of steam in 1912, Dr. Joseph Damiani, its president, told the *Chicago Record-Herald* that they were "so discouraged by the lax administration of justice that they were refusing to advance further money to prosecute men arrested on their complaints."[202] The White Hand couldn't defeat both the Black Hand and a corrupt Chicago justice system.

Not long after the White Hand was founded in Chicago, a branch was organized in Pittsburgh as well. The leaders were Joseph Sunseri, a fruit wholesaler and the wealthiest Italian in the city; Ernest Bisi, a wholesale grocer and producer of macaroni; and Mariana Cancelleri, editor of the local Italian newspaper. Early in December, both Sunseri and Bisi were recipients of Black Hand letters threatening them with death (being shot in the head and heart) if they did not pay $1,000 each in tribute. Bisi's letter instructed him to meet members of the Black Hand at the Baltimore & Ohio station on December 8, 1907. So he notified the county detectives of the planned rendezvous, and it was arranged for twenty officers to be on hand for it. However, the Black Hand did not show up. Sunseri's letter directed him to deliver the money to the produce yards the following afternoon, December 10. Taking matters into his own hands, Sunseri armed himself with a new revolver and recruited a half dozen of his friends to accompany him.

When he reached the produce yard, Sunseri was met by M. Rei (or Reis) and Joseph Colandio or Caruso (aka Joe Gemite or John Gomite), who suggested he step inside a railroad car to inspect some fruit. When he did so, the two men demanded that he surrender the money. Instead, Sunseri fired his revolver, signaling his companions to come to his assistance. It is believed that Colandio shot Sunseri first and then took off with Sunseri in hot pursuit. Despite being seriously wounded, Sunseri was able to discharge his own weapon, striking both Colandio and Rei. Though shot through the cheek, Colandio was still fighting when the police rescued him from a score of citizens who were preparing to lynch him.

Other witnesses testified that Rei, Colandio and two other men entered a railroad car in which Sunseri was selling bananas. When they began to quarrel over the prices, Sunseri shot Rei in self-defense. The other men quickly produced knives and revolvers, and the two sides engaged in a shootout. "The fight spread out of the produce yards and down Pennsylvania Avenue for three blocks, when the arrival of the police reserves put an end to the battle."[203] Some twenty men took part, and hundreds of shots were fired.

Police reserves from three station houses had to be called out to quell the riot. In its aftermath, Sunseri lay seriously wounded in the West Penn Hospital; Rei, alleged leader of the Black Hand, was dying in the same hospital; and Colandio was recovering in the police hospital.

Four years later, there were rumors of a new White Hand in Pittsburgh. Again, it was believed to be composed of all well-to-do Italians who had armed themselves to protect life and property if necessary. According to the *Pittsburgh Gazette Times*, Magistrate Joseph Natali was supportive of the idea of peace-loving members of the community organizing a secret society to work separately from the police to combat the Black Hand.

Although branches of the White Hand would occasionally make themselves known in various cities throughout the United States—Reading, Pennsylvania; New York City; St. Louis, Missouri; Wilmington, Delaware; Hazelton, Pennsylvania—they were not all that effective in protecting Italians from assorted Black Hand crimes. So in July 1908, Lloyd's of London stepped into the breach and began issuing "a new form of freak insurance."[204] As many victims were learning to their dismay, fire insurance did not cover the dynamiting of buildings unless a fire resulted. Recognizing a need, Lloyd's created so-called Black Hand insurance policies at an average rate of 5 percent. And it wasn't just for Black Hand crimes. Bomb-throwing anarchists dated back to the 1886 Haymarket Square riot in Chicago but would be propelled back into the public consciousness in March 1908, when they hit New York's Union Square.[205]

There were some fake White Hand societies as well. In January 1908, Eugene Fair sent Mrs. M.E. Parmenter of Columbus, Kansas, an extortion letter, demanding $500 under penalty of death. Curiously, he wrote, "We knew you in Ohio" and signed the letter "The White Hand Society."[206] Fair, who was well known to the Columbus police, was arrested by the local Anti-Horse Thief Association. Then in July 1909, Nicholas Conti fled to Toledo, Ohio, with his nine-year-old daughter, Lillian, in tow and begged the police to protect him from the White Hand. He claimed the organization had driven him out of Chicago and that one of its agents had followed them on the train.[207]

If there were any White Hand groups formed in Ohio, they kept quiet about it. However, in July 1909, when the Black Hand troubles were at their peak in the Buckeye State, the White Hand Society of Chicago contacted Postal Inspector J.F. Oldfield, offering to do whatever they could to assist him with his investigation. And they sent him a copy of their book.

# 11

# SAFE IN HELLTOWN

*Only in Pennsylvania has a means been found of curtailing the murderous activities of the terrible organization which under the name of "Black Hand," has been committing outrages all over the United States.*[208]
—Cook County Herald

So many Italians migrated to Pennsylvania that they became the second largest ethnic group in the state during the first half of the twentieth century. Although 90 percent of Italian immigrants settled in major cities nationwide, 71 percent of those who came to Pennsylvania gravitated to the smaller industrial communities. As a result, these areas experienced their share of Italian crime, and a connection between the Pennsylvania gangs and the ones in Ohio was theorized, especially along the Pennsylvania-Ohio border.

On Sunday night, September 2, 1906, a bloody battle took place at Pennsylvania's Florence mine, seven miles from Punxsutawney, pitting as many as twenty-six members of Troop D of the state police against a gang of "foreigners."[209] "The trouble began at 3 o'clock in the afternoon, when Sergt. [Joseph] Logan went to Florence to search for Leopold Scarlatz, who [was] charged with shooting his brother-in-law."[210]

While Logan was standing in Dr. Bodenhorn's office, dressed in civilian clothes, a fight broke out in the street between Salvatore Waltzoch and a fellow countryman. The officer promptly arrested Waltzoch, who asked him to come into the boardinghouse so he could prove his good character.

Many immigrant children worked in Pennsylvania coal mines. *Library of Congress.*

Once inside, Logan had to fend off a man who lunged at him with a stiletto. He then retreated some fifteen feet before the Italian fired at him with a shotgun. Pulling his own revolver, the two men shot it out. Logan was struck in the foot with buckshot, but his attacker fell back into the house, wounded and possibly dead.

Telephoning for assistance, Logan was assigned a detachment of five soldiers, who arrived in Florence on the trolley at 4:30 p.m. Deciding to charge the house, all five men were quickly mown down by the Italians. "Realizing that lives were being sacrificed uselessly, and the storm and darkness being on, the troopers, who had been using only their side arms, sent for their carbines and prepared to keep the house surrounded until morning."[211] Logan called for more help, and fifteen additional troopers arrived at 6:30 p.m. They were joined by the local police, and a furious gun battle ensued. Under the cover of darkness, the officers fired volley after volley into the building. Some five hundred to one thousand shots were exchanged as the rain fell in torrents.

Finally, at dawn, the police placed twenty pounds of dynamite under the building. "It went off with fearful effect, shattering one side of the house and breaking numerous windows in the houses roundabout."[212] The resulting fire reduced it to a pile of ashes by 8:30 Monday morning. Only one man was found inside, Jim Timbone, a gun and ammunition at his side. It was believed that others had escaped during the night. A local paper reported that Florence was the headquarters for a Black Hand gang. "Since the fight, however, the coolest heads have arrived at the opinion that there never was more than three Italians in the house after the firing commenced and possibly only one, the desperate Timbone."[213]

In all, two troopers were killed, a third mortally wounded and three others injured by three different guns. Eight suspects were rounded up, all Italians and all carrying concealed weapons. If these men were engaged in Black Hand–style extortion attempts, it was not mentioned. However, just after Christmas, Antonio Moreno "was found unconscious and weltering in a pool of blood near an Italian boarding house on the outskirts of Washington," Pennsylvania, more than one hundred miles southwest of Florence.[214] While on his death bed, he said that five members of the Black Hand had stabbed him from behind. He had previously received letters ordering him to pay tribute by leaving money at designated drop spots but repeatedly refused.

On the opposite side of the state, twenty-two men went on trial in Wilkes-Barre in April 1907 on a variety of charges purportedly connected with the Black Hand. There were thirteen counts of shooting with intent to kill, thirteen of conspiracy, a half dozen for dynamiting and two of robbery by threats and menacing. The defendants had been exposed by Charles Salvatore and Joseph Ritz of Brownstown, who had received a letter demanding payment of $500 or else they and their families would be slain. Testimony subsequently revealed, "Hundreds of foreign families in this section [had] for several years lived in a state bordering in terror as a result of threats made by this mysterious organization, which in many cases have been followed up with murder."[215]

Believed to be an offshoot of New York and Philadelphia Black Hand societies, it was purportedly led by Louis "Ox" Perino of the Pittsburgh suburb of Brownstown until his death at the hands of an assassin.[216] He had introduced a band of "strange Italians from the large cities" to the most prosperous Italians in the area and soon thereafter they began receiving Black Hand letters, threatening their lives if they did not pay tribute.[217] Since the victims believed Perino was their friend, they would go to him for help, and he would negotiate a 50 percent settlement with the blackmailers on the condition that they would not be bothered further. However, he would then keep the larger portion of the payoffs for himself. "This led to a quarrel with his lieutenants and one night he was shot down in the roadway."[218] Those victims of the extortionists who did not agree to a settlement arranged by Perino either died—three murders took place—or were subject to robbery.

The Commonwealth of Pennsylvania charged that there was a "conspiracy within a conspiracy" and that witnesses had been intimidated into not identifying the Black Hand suspects.[219] One of them, Joseph Norcatzzi, admitted he had received threatening letters and, fearing his life was in danger, moved to Buffalo, New York. Another, Salvatore Scannoca, eventually pointed out Charles Lucchini as the man to whom he had paid fifty dollars.

Even in major cities, law enforcement did not have adequate manpower to bring to bear on many alleged Black Hand crimes, so sometimes major corporations took matters into their own hands. The *Fairmont West Virginian* reported, "After working for months, spending thousands of dollars and spreading a dragnet that has caught men in four States, the United States Steel Corporation has rounded up what officers say is the worst gang of Black Hand in the country."[220]

By the end of July, dozens of men had been jailed in New Castle and Sharon, Pennsylvania; Plainfield, New Jersey; Rochester, New York; and Youngstown, Ohio. In response, several constables and police officers received death threats. The Mercer County, Pennsylvania commissioners decided to conduct their own independent investigation. They hired two detectives to track down the killers of two county residents since U.S. Steel had no vested interest in these crimes. At least a dozen murders in the Mahoning and Shenandoah Valleys were attributed to the Black Hand over two years. Blackmailed citizens had withdrawn so much money from local banks that it was causing an economic hardship in the community.

Having operated with impunity for several years, the Black Handers at Hillsville (known locally as "Helltown") were not easily intimidated. The town stood on a height from which the smoke from furnaces in New Castle, Youngstown and Sharon could be seen. Impenetrable woods surrounded it. The Johnston Limestone Quarries offered the gang many caverns in which they could hide out. According to one newspaper, "A fugitive from justice was as safe in 'Helltown' as in the moon."[221] Few law officers dared to venture into the area. And actionable evidence was hard to come by because people feared repercussions.

Detective Creighton G. Logan of Lawrence County, Pennsylvania; Chief W.W. McDowell of Youngstown, Ohio; and a group of Pinkerton detectives (including Dimaio) employed by U.S. Steel joined forces in a raid. "In one afternoon, twenty-one men were arrested at Hillsville and taken to New

Most Black Hand gangs were strictly local like this one in Fairmount, West Virginia. *Library of Congress.*

Castle jail, on charges of conspiracy to rob and being suspicious persons."[222] Only then did the victims feel free to tell their stories. However, few of the men arrested were thought to be actual members of the gang but were pressured to commit crimes by those who were.

One of the suspects was John Jotti (or Joti or Jati), who conducted a school for fencing. It was actually believed to be a school for assassins in which Jotti taught young Black Handers how to efficiently dispatch someone with a stiletto, practicing on a rubber mannequin that was marked to show the places that would produce instant death. (Detective Dimaio purportedly took a few lessons from him while working undercover.) Jotti had been arrested in Youngstown in July and charged with several counts of extorting money. He was subsequently offered "a good salary" to appear in vaudeville. The *Marion Daily Mirror* had mused, "It is possible that for the public weal it would be preferable for John to continue his work as a Black Hand agent."[223]

Picked up in the east end of Youngstown, Jotti and Giuseppe Catronico (aka Joe Constrano) were "supposed to be ringleaders of the gang that has terrorized not only Italians living in Youngstown, but also in the western part of Pennsylvania."[224] One witness, Nicolo Clurieo, related that he had been suspected of being a detective. Taken by force to a house in Hillsville, he was hauled before thirty or forty men. When he refused to join their gang, he was stripped naked. "The men formed a ring around him and as they danced around each one would spit in his face and strike him."[225] Because he continued to resist, they dunked him in a tub of water until he nearly drowned before turning him loose.

Forty-two Italians were rounded up on August 3, 1907, in Marion Heights, Pennsylvania, on suspicion of being members of a Black Hand society. The previous month, there had been "a carnival of crimes…with scores of robberies and a dozen murders."[226] Previous efforts by the county constables to arrest the suspects had been frustrated by failure to find witnesses to testify owing to fear of death.

A few days before the arrests, several Italian detectives learned that the local Black Hand gang was planning to assassinate various people who had been lodging complaints against the Black Handers with the justice of the peace. This spurred the law officers to make a coordinated effort to take them into custody. However, several of the leaders had escaped their dragnet.

Situated in Northumberland County, Marion Heights was a notoriously lawless area of the state. In 1908, the *Bloomsburg Columbian* reported that in the past fifteen years, ninety-seven murders had been committed in the region, but only five men had been tried and only one was ultimately convicted of first-degree murder.

Several months later, a fight broke out between two men in the village of Marion Heights. Nick Gedro was shot five times by Andrea Yunado, an alleged member of the Black Hand. As soon as Gedro recovered from his wounds, he set out to even the score with his stiletto. However, he was arrested as soon as he stepped out of the hospital and charged with stabbing William Murdon on March 7 and assaulting Charles Fetterman on August 4 in the town of Centralia. No one knew what had become of him until they read about the shooting in the newspapers.

In October 1907, twenty-three Italians were sentenced to prison at New Castle for Black Hand crimes.[227] By the following month, newspapers were trumpeting the Keystone State's success in quashing the criminal organization. "Only in Pennsylvania," the *Cook County Herald* proclaimed, "has a means been found of curtailing the murderous activities of the terrible organization which under the name of 'Black Hand,' has been committing outrages all over the United States."[228] It failed to mention that a private company—U.S. Steel—had been instrumental in accomplishing the feat.

While New York seemed powerless to prevent near daily murders and the post office was struggling to find a way to keep from being an unwitting agent, Pennsylvania was attacking the problem through its state constabulary. The first instance of the Black Hand in Pennsylvania had involved a company of miners made to pay tribute, so the state was able to draw on its experience in stamping out the Molly Maguires thirty years before. In that case, a Pinkerton detective was able to infiltrate the Irish group. With the evidence he collected, eleven were hanged. This time, a member of the state police was able to enter the Italian organization and do the same. But, like an underground coal fire, it appeared to be extinguished only to erupt elsewhere, days, weeks or months later.

On a Sunday afternoon late in May 1909, Joe Zappe was shot and killed by Raffaele Capputo while walking down the street in Wireton, Pennsylvania. A month earlier, Capputo had received a Black Hand letter demanding payment of $200 and he had been robbed of $20 by three men. When their paths crossed, Capputo refused to give Zappe the $20 he wanted and instead shot three times with his own revolver—while it was still in his coat pocket, setting fire to it. Each bullet struck the thirty-eight-year-old Zappe in the lungs. Apparently, Zappe and his friends all fired at Capputo as he fled but did not hit him. However, Capputo was soon apprehended by the police. They then went to Zappe's boardinghouse in nearby Monessen and arrested all of the residents. Zappe was suspected of belonging to a Black Hand gang that had demanded $200 from Mike Gilda, a local merchant.

# 12

# DEATH ON THE DOORSTEP

*Don't you sons-of-bitches move or I'll shoot your damn heads off.*[229]
— *Salvatore Presutti*

On New Year's Day 1909, Mrs. John Amicon noticed a parcel on the back porch of her home at 579 East Rich Street, Columbus, Ohio. It was a bomb. Wrapped around a few sticks of dynamite was a sheet of paper that read:

*Mr. John and Charlie:*

*We wish $10,000, $5,000 from each. Therefore search for friends to bring this sum to Pittsburg at once, if you value your life. This which you found is a sample, but if you go to the police you are lost. Therefore consult with the other members of the family before you act, for the law cannot watch you the year around. Therefore do not confide in anyone, but think of your wives and children.*

*THE EXTERMINATION.*[230]

The explosives did not go off and, apparently, were not intended to. Mrs. Amicon would continue to live in the same house until her death thirty-two-years later.

Salvatore Presutti was the proprietor of the First and Last Chance Saloon. *Columbus Metropolitan Library.*

At the time, protection rackets were not uncommon, as Salvatore Presutti could attest. Having signed on with Ringling Brothers in New York, he found himself just outside Columbus when the circus ended its run. With few options to choose from, he took a job as a porter in a local spaghetti house. He was sixteen. Three years later, an agent of the Hoster-Columbus Associated Breweries approached him with the opportunity to run his own saloon. Presutti secured a liquor license and opened the First and Last Chance Saloon at 519 West Goodale Street in 1908.

Located on the western edge of Flytown, Presutti's barroom served one of the city's worst neighborhoods. (Flytown residents had once complained about inmates from the nearby Ohio Penitentiary—trustees of a sort—roaming the streets, drinking beer and getting into fights, all while still decked out in prison stripes.) Not surprisingly, some of the toughest men in Columbus walked through Presutti's doors. To help maintain decorum, Presutti hired bare-knuckle fighter Fritz Wentzell as his bouncer.

When some of the saloon's customers got into brawls, which they inevitably did, Fritz would toss them out into the street. And if brute strength wasn't enough, Presutti would pull out the .38-caliber revolver he kept stashed under the counter. Such was the life of a small-time businessman in Ohio's capital.

"Papa" Presutti, as he would later be known, was accustomed to petty thugs trying to hit him up for money or beer, but as his business became more successful, he attracted the attention of a criminal element somewhat higher up in the food chain—those selling protection. Typically, some ruffian would enter a business, swagger up to the cash register and help himself to whatever was in the till. If the owner protested, he was shoved out of the way or worse. For the most part, the victims remained silent, fearing retribution if they complained. But Presutti wasn't afraid to mix it up when necessary.

One day, a nameless hooligan entered the First and Last Chance Saloon, grabbed the day's receipts from the cash register and sauntered out. As he was climbing on the back of a waiting motorcycle, Presutti charged out the door, pistol in hand. "Don't you sons-of-bitches move or I'll shoot your damn heads off," he shouted, pressing the barrel of the gun against the man's head. "That money is mine. I've got to buy beer and whiskey, pay my bills. Give it to me."[231] After handing Presutti's money back to him, the thief fled on the motorcycle, never to return.

Presutti apparently did not experience further interference from local gangsters—nothing worth mentioning, anyway. But other Italians did. And it had moved beyond the strong-arm robbery stage. Two weeks after Mrs. Amicon discovered a bomb, Francesca, a niece who resided with the family, found a second one. She was heading off for school on the morning of January 15, 1909, when she spotted a package on the front doorstep. It was loosely wrapped in a copy of the *Pittsburg Dispatch*. The girl carried it into the house and showed it to Mrs. Amicon, who recognized it as another bomb. Although both were alarmed, they placed it in a pan, covered it with water and carried it to the barn. Later that afternoon when he returned from work, John Amicon transported the bomb to a sporting goods store, where it was found to be packed with dynamite.

But bombs were nothing new to Columbus. Eight months earlier, on the morning of May 13, 1908, someone had attempted to dynamite the Mt. Vernon Avenue home of Agostino "Gus" Iannarino. "About 3 o'clock the eight people occupying the house were all thrown out of bed by a terrific explosion of dynamite placed on the steps."[232] The lower part of the dwelling was a mass of splinters, and all the windows were shattered. Luckily, no one was harmed.

A month earlier, the Iannarinos had received several letters, the first demanding $10,000 and the others $2,000 (or $3,000), threatening to blow up their house if they did not pay. Two weeks later, the brothers closed up shop, sold three houses, withdrew $16,000 from the bank and left with their families—fifteen people in all—for Boston. They feared that harm would befall their children or their wives if they remained in Columbus. Accompanying them was Sergeant Churches of the Columbus Police Department. He would ensure they made it safely on board a ship for Italy.

Originally, the Iannarinos intended to remain abroad until the Black Hand troubles subsided. But despite the dangers, unhappiness with the conditions there induced them to return to Columbus in May 1909. Gus explained that another Black Hand letter had found him while he was in Trabia, Italy. The handwriting and the paper were purportedly identical to those mailed to him in Columbus. As many Italians were learning, you could run, but you couldn't hide. And now their fellow fruit vendors, the Amicons, were being targeted.

Giovanni Carmen "John" Amicon (shortened from Amicone) was born in Campobello, Forli, Italy, on October 16, 1867. He came to the United States at the age of fifteen and became a citizen on March 27, 1889. John married Theresa Rosasco of Genoa, Italy. His elder brother Carlo "Charles" Amicon would marry Maria Bova a little later.

About 1884, John settled in Chillicothe, Ohio, where he and his brother began selling fruit, candy, ice cream and cigars out of a tiny storeroom on West Second Street opposite the post office.[233] Over the course of a dozen years, they built a thriving business. Then in 1896, John sold out to Andrew and Joseph Amicon (relationship unknown) and, along with Charles and their families, relocated to Columbus, fifty miles to the north. His plan was to become a wholesale fruit seller.

"At that time," a history of the Catholic diocese recorded, "the Italian congregation was very small and, we may say, poor."[234] Discouraged, the priest quit. But not the Amicons. Within a decade, John and Charles (but not a third brother, Anthony) were operating John Amicon Brothers & Company out of a four-story building at the southwest corner of Third and Naghten Streets, adjacent to the railroad yards.[235] "The Banana Kings," as they called themselves, also had facilities in Boardman, Michigan; Bluefield, West Virginia; Parkersburg, West Virginia; Seneca Castle, New York; and Springfield, Marion and Carey, Ohio. They handled twenty-five carloads of bananas every week and claimed to receive more shipments of California and Florida oranges than any other single produce house in the country.

John and Charles had become wealthy—generating more than $1 million in sales annually—and, like most men of wealth, they could afford to be generous. Along with Charles Segale and ten other prominent Italian businessmen of the city—bankers, manufacturers, grocers—John had

The Amicon brothers' letterhead depicted the extent of their produce empire. *Authors' collection.*

pledged to support the Ellery Band, which they hoped to book for regular Sunday concerts. However, when the letters started arriving, threatening him and his family with death and destruction if he did not pay tribute, John Amicon ignored them.

But ignoring a bomb on the doorstep was another matter altogether. John decided to take this latest letter to the Italian ambassador, who subsequently handed it over to postal inspectors. As far as the bomb itself was concerned, R. Herman Holland, the American representative of the Amicon Brothers, placed it in the magazine of the Columbus Sporting Goods Company for safekeeping.[236] Not long afterward, the building caught fire and the bomb exploded, blowing the building to pieces.

Post Office inspector J. Frank Oldfield was the detective assigned to the Amicon investigation. As the *New York Times* noted, "When a city police department undertakes to run down a crime it proceeds according to certain well-sanctioned methods, and if it does not discover the criminal in a certain length of time it drops the case."[237] However, the detective had the time and resources to spend months or years on a case.

In the days that followed, Anthony Ricciardio, a well-to-do fruit dealer and confectioner, was found hacked to death in his store in Scranton, Pennsylvania—likely a victim of the Black Hand. And a couple of weeks after that, six members of an alleged Black Hand organization were arrested in Ellsworth, Pennsylvania, following "a desperate hand-to-hand battle with eight officers."[238] Closer to home, Antonio Guanni, a fruit dealer in Canton, Ohio, received a Black Hand letter, demanding payment of $1,000. Although these incidents were reported in Columbus newspapers, it is not known whether the Amicon brothers took any note of them. But it would have been hard to overlook what was taking place in their own backyard.

A month to the day later, Peter Jetka, an Italian fruit vendor of East Naghten Street, notified Columbus police that he had paid $1,000 to the Black Hand rather than incur their anger. His neighbor, grocer Ignas Farson, had received such letters and "told the police he had been waiting for representatives of the blackmailing organization to call on him for money, which he was willing to pay to insure his safety."[239] Initially, they had demanded $2,000, but later letters asked for smaller amounts. For reasons they didn't go into, the police suspected that the perpetrators were not Columbus residents.

While someone was putting the squeeze on Italians in Columbus, a poster was found tacked to a tree in the Marion courthouse esplanade on the morning of February 13. It announced, "We, 70 Americans, bonded together by death to keep the secret, notify you that unless the poor are given food, we will burn the whole town in the night. Beware, your lives are at stake."[240] The Marion police had no clues as to the identity of those responsible or even if they were serious. But it was unsettling in its own way.

The would-be blackmailers of the Amicon brothers soon followed up with another letter:

*Dear friend John*

*The last month you found dynamite and a letter back of your door, also your brother found one, and you are ordered by our band to pay $10,000.00. Afterwards we sent a letter to your brother where he was to look for some honorable persons that were to bring the money to Pittsburg, Pa., where our leaders lives. Three persons were to walk around in said city. In the meantime while they were walking around, they would be found by us. This was to be before the tenth of February. This day passed, and we saw nobody walking around. Poor people that you have made your calculations wrong. We have already selected two young men that are obligated to butcher you at the cost of our lives. Read the newspapers well, and see what we have done in New York, New Orleans and Chicago, and other cities. You will understand that under our hand nobody has escaped. Neither will you. It will be awful for you if you turn to the police. You understand that the police cannot watch you all the time, even if they could, instead of two we will be 10 or 20, and if you were in the midst of 1000 police, the first rifle shot would be for you, and afterwards all of the police would die who are watching you. We are a multitude, brave shots, that one time in a* *mountain met lots of police and killed 20 and the rest ran, and we were only four. So you see, we kill who do not obey our commands, and do not fear the police. We have riffles that will make you shiver. We don't want to do much talking. Make your calculations good. You are compelled to leave your business if you come to your duty we will make you be respected by the whole world. We exist everywhere, and all are under our feet. See what you have resolved as soon as you get this. Hunt honorable persons, give them the money, and they will come to Pittsburg, and while they will be hunting, they will be found by us, and there cannot be over two. Do your calculations, and don't think of it because you can see yourself in the hands of the lion. Money to you is nothing. Come to your duty. Come with your money or your life. If you are deaf, in a few days we will eat your heart, miserable that you are.*

*THE BLACK HAND*
*HAND OF THE DEVIL.*

*Your Place.*[241]

The *New York Sun* published a story on February 20, 1909, detailing New York police lieutenant Joseph Petrosino's upcoming trip to Sicily. It was intended to be a secret investigation. When Commissioner Bingham was asked where Petrosino was, he replied in his typically blunt manner, "Why he may be on the ocean bound for Europe for all I know"—effectively blowing his cover. Other newspapers published similar stories. Twenty days later, Petrosino was murdered in the town of Palermo.

The previous December, Petrosino had been promoted to lieutenant as a result of the Bingham Bill, the first native-born Italian to achieve that rank on any police force in the nation.[242] Commissioner Bingham had lobbied for the law to give him the powers he needed to institute reforms in the New York Police Department. And Petrosino and the Italian Unit was a key component in his plans.

Unlike many members of law enforcement, Petrosino had no doubt that the Mafia was real. He just didn't think it was here in the United States. To help him better understand it, he decided to take a firsthand look, arriving in Palermo on March 12, 1909. It was believed that Petrosino was engaged in tracking down two men who had returned to Sicily from America and participated in the looting of Messina following the recent earthquake. When he approached some friends of the suspects, they "decided to put

In *Black Hand*, Hollywood depicted the murder of New York Police lieutenant Petrosino. *Authors' collection.*

him out of the way."[243] An unnamed informant sent him a message, asking that he meet him in the city's Piazza Marina, where he would give him some inside information on the criminal organization. However, it was a trap.

While waiting to meet his contact, the forty-eight-year-old Petrosino was fired on by a group of assassins. His killers were never identified. Don Vito Cascioferro, who had returned to Sicily from the United States in 1904, is considered by some to have been the likely architect of Petrosino's death. Two men were seen running from the scene of the crime, and legend has it, one of them was Cascioferro. He purportedly arranged for an alibi with a highly placed friend, then drove to the center of Palermo to await the appearance of Petrosino. After shooting the lawman down, Cascioferro returned to the home of the friend who provided him with an alibi. While this is unlikely, the two men—Cascioferro and Petrosino—did bear each other considerable enmity. Petrosino was purportedly carrying a note in which Cascioferro was described as "a terrible criminal," while Cascioferro kept a photograph of his nemesis.[244]

Petrosino's assassination sparked a nationwide crackdown—dubbed by some as a "war of extermination"—on the Black Hand and the Camorra. Hundreds of suspects were rounded up throughout Italy. The people of Sicily were in an uproar over the failure of their government and the police to apprehend the responsible persons. A rumor began to make the rounds that he was killed by Mafia members from Caltanisetta who were aligned with Failla Mulone, a noted brigand. At the time, Mulone was in America, but it was believed Petrosino was arranging for his extradition to Sicily.

At police headquarters in New York, there "was a feeling of chagrin and even resentment over the fact not one word regarding the murder of the noted New York detective" Petrosino had been communicated to them, despite having sent a cable asking for it.[245] Inspector James McCafferty, head of the detective bureau, remarked, "If an Italian detective sent here on a mission by that government and working in behalf of the Italian police had been murdered in New York, we would have notified the slain man's home department at once."[246]

McCafferty was especially interested in learning whether Petrosino had been robbed; he had some valuable documents in his possession which, if they fell into the wrong hands, would reveal the department's plan regarding the Italian criminals. As Petrosino's heir apparent, Lieutenant Vachris, accompanied by two detectives, was dispatched to Italy. He was to retrieve Petrosino's records and conduct his own investigation of the assassination.

Italian authorities did not know whom to blame for Petrosino's death. It could have been the Mafia or the Black Hand or, possibly, a gang of international forgers that had been picked up in Florence the previous month—or, it was later suggested, a couple of Black Handers in Ohio. Dispatches from Palermo indicated that a Mafia secret council had issued orders warning everyone, including newspaper editors, to avoid discussing his death too freely or mentioning any names.

## 13

# BRING A LIVE CHICKEN

*They are a dangerous band and should be exterminated.*[247]
— *U.S. Attorney William Day*

J ohn Frank Oldfield was regarded as one of the United States Postal
Inspection Service's top investigators. Born in Ellicott City, Maryland,
Oldfield had started in Republican politics early in his life and became
sheriff of Howard County at about the age of thirty. He joined the United
States Postal Inspection Office during the administration of President
William McKinley, working primarily in the Midwest. The oldest law
enforcement agency in the country, the USPIS was also the most powerful,
and forty-three-year-old Oldfield knew how to marshal its considerable
resources for lengthy and far-ranging criminal investigations—the kind that
local police forces didn't have the ability to tackle.

Among Oldfield's most famous cases was one involving a former
congressman who was convicted of taking bribes for the purchase of postage
stamp machines. Oldfield also got the goods on a handful of embezzling
postmasters, as well as some gamblers and pornographers. Along the way,
his career had survived a few mishaps, most notably when he was accused of
releasing two prisoners from jail so they could register to vote. But now he
was on the trail of what would prove to be his biggest quarry—the ubiquitous
Black Hand.

It was widely reported that Oldfield began looking into the Black Hand
on March 1, 1909, prompted by the discovery of a bomb planted at John

*From left to right*: Postal Inspectors J.F. Oldfield, R.M.C. Hosford and George Pate. *Library of Congress.*

Amicon's house two months earlier. However, by the time the case came to trial, he was saying he had begun the previous August when "he first learned that Black Hand letters were being circulated in the district."[248] At least one newspaper suggested the investigation may have actually commenced following the Iannarino bombing nearly a year earlier. If so, there had been little progress until the Amicon family was involved.

A major break in the case came about when Detective Dimaio of the Pinkertons notified Oldfield that the headquarters of the Society of the Banana and Faithful Friends—as the gang named itself—was in Marion, Ohio, and a meeting of its members had been called for March 9. Pittsburgh police had recently arrested twenty-one suspected Black Hand members, and Dimaio had participated in their interrogation. (Seven years before, the detective was described as "undoubtedly a grand master of the sweating process"—possibly including waterboarding.)[249] Considered Petrosino's equal in his knowledge of Italian gangs, Dimaio persuaded one of the suspects to rat out his comrades. He learned that some members of the society were so upset over the division of the spoils that they decided to convene a meeting in Marion to discuss it. The man's confession "gave the government agents all the secrets and information" they needed to begin closing in on the suspects.[250]

In advance of the meeting, Oldfield dispatched a team of inspectors—E.F. Hutches, George Pate and R.M.C. Hosford—from Cincinnati to Marion to see what they could learn. Hosford, in particular, was a doggedly determined investigator who had previously worked in Kansas and Oklahoma. His tenure, however, had not been without controversy. He was accused of stealing post office funds, assaulting a woman and forcing a false confession. Hutches and Pate had been rural free delivery inspectors.[251]

"The federal men...obtained a building adjoining the fruit store of Sam Lima and through a hole in the wall watched the conference of the plotters."[252] They also observed a number of men disembarking at the railroad station and making their way to Salvatore Lima's fruit stand at 235 North Main Street. And later that day, they witnessed the delivery of a load of cots to the store.

Keeping the meeting under surveillance throughout the night, the agents ascertained the names of all the men in attendance—more than twenty. From that day on, every letter sent from Lima's store was tracked. Each money order was recorded. Stamps were specially marked, and the local postmaster was instructed to sell them only to Salvatore Lima and his brother Sebastiano. In this way, Oldfield's men were able to trace the continuing flow of letters turned over to Postmaster Krumm by John and Charles Amicon. One letter from Lima's store in Marion went to Augustino (aka Agostino) Marfisi in Dennison and then to Antonio Vicarrio before it was delivered to the Amicons.[253] A second letter traveled by way of Cleveland. Some were transported as far as Washington State for mailing.

No doubt Oldfield was pleased with how his investigation was progressing. However, in April, newspapers reported "a placard, written in blood, was posted on a tree near the Marion courthouse," bearing "a threat to burn the city unless investigation into the operations of Italians were stopped."[254] Although they had lost the element of surprise, Oldfield's men were forced to bide their time.

As the postal inspectors continued gathering evidence, the funeral of Lieutenant Petrosino was taking place—one of the largest in Manhattan history. On April 12, a bright sunlit day, over seven thousand people marched in the procession, and a quarter of a million others turned out to pay their respects to their fallen hero. At the very least, Petrosino's death added fuel to the debate on whether there was an overarching Black Hand Society.

At about the same time Petrosino sailed for Italy, three Italians had departed from New Orleans on two different steamers "and should have reached Palermo previous to Petrosino's assassination."[255] When the trio returned through the port of New York, they caught the attention of the New York City police department. But they would not be the only suspects. As Inspector Oldfield carried out his own investigation, the thought surely crossed his mind that, perhaps, he would find a link between the Society of the Banana and Petrosino's murder.

Detective Peter Angelo of Pittsburgh knew Petrosino personally and had held him in high esteem. He believed that the Black Hand Society was real and not just a smokescreen used by unrelated bands of criminals. As proof, he offered the case of Tresca, the editor of an Italian newspaper, who was cut by a stranger acting on orders from someone else. Angelo also had a set of bylaws he had confiscated the year before when he arrested some Italians in Sewickley. "These by-laws, printed in the newspapers at the time, were blood-thirsty ordinances of a secret band of assassins, who threatened death for every violation of their infamous pact."[256]

Nevertheless, on April 16, 1909, Bernard Berasa, former attorney for the Italian consul in Chicago, declared that the Black Hand was a myth harming criminal proceedings. "When I go into court to try a case before a jury I have to ask the veniremen [prospective jurors] whether they are prejudiced

Many of the alleged gang members were seen arriving at the railroad depot in Marion. *Authors' collection.*

gainst Italians. I find that hundreds of men are. A little questioning brings out the face that this prejudice is founded on the Black Hand stories.[257] He insisted that wealthy Italians in Chicago never received extortion letters. "Now, I personally have investigated fully twenty of these alleged Black Hand outrages, and in every instance I found either that the people were not Italians or that the whole thing was a fake."[258] While that may have been Berasa's experience—that none of the culprits were Italian—it did not seem to hold true for much of the country outside of Chicago.

Black Hand–like activities throughout Ohio and adjoining states continued unabated. The challenge confronting Oldfield and his team was finding the connections. He already had pins in his map for Columbus, Marion and Pittsburgh. But what about the others? For example, at the beginning of April, an unidentified attorney in Fremont, Ohio, received a Black Hand letter written in French. It demanded $1,000 or else the lawyer's head would be blown off. He was placed under police protection. And not long afterward, a Cleveland councilman, Charles L. Selzer of the Sixth Ward, received a letter threatening to kill his nineteen-year-old son, Frank, if he did not pay the writer $500. Selzer turned the letter over to the police, who assigned a guard to the teenager while an investigation was conducted. Was this the work of an individual or a group? Was it a onetime attempt at blackmail or part of a series?

In Springfield, Henry Kempler was warned "that he must distribute $1000 in money or provisions among the poor white and colored people living near his grocery" by April 20 or his home would be dynamited.[259] The letter specified that the intended beneficiaries were poor people who could not patronize his store because they did not have the money. At about the same time, Joseph Spangenberger, a wealthy manufacturer of soft drinks, received a Black Hand letter demanding $500 and "that he dispense charity to his poor neighbors, both white and black, upon pain of death and destruction of property."[260] And Julius Orahs, a wealthy butcher, was ordered to pay $500 by April 27.

Helen Ayers, an African American teenager, was arrested and confessed to writing a number of the Black Hand letters. A marked postage stamp led to her capture. She said she had been reading detective stories and did it for fun. However, on April 26, the shoe firm of Stimmel & Powers received a letter demanding that $500 be left in Springfield's Snyder Park by May 2 or employees' homes and the business would be destroyed. The letter was written on the same stationery used by Ayers but in different handwriting, leading the police to believe that a friend of hers had created it.

The same month, "much distress [was] being brought about among the Italians employed by the Erie railroad in and about [Marion] and especially near Galion by the threats of the Black Hand society."[261] A number of newly arrived immigrants were attempting to extort money from the railroad employees, using the familiar Black Hand methods. Many of the workers readily surrendered their money to the thugs and were suffering from want of food.

Also in April, Joseph Gugliotti presented himself at Braddock Bank in Pittsburgh, accompanied by two "foreign" gentlemen. He asked to withdraw $300. The teller noted that Gugliotti was bleeding and called for an interpreter. Guigliotto then revealed that the two—Salvator Roberto and Nicolo Digliotti—had cut strips of flesh from his breast because he had refused to pay them money. The men were promptly arrested and held for police.

At their hearing, Gugliotti related that he had received several Black Hand letters demanding payment, which he ignored. When he woke up that day, he found Roberto and Digliotti standing over him. They demanded $300, and when he wouldn't give it to him, one of them pulled a stiletto and slashed his arms and face. "Still he said he refused to comply with their demands until one of them began carving pieces out of his breast."[262] His wounds bandaged, but weak from loss of blood, Gugliotti agreed to go to the bank.

Inspector Oldfield and Postmaster Krumm would soon become good friends, if they weren't already. Stretched thin by the sheer volume of Black Hand activity flaring up all over the Midwest, they were able to call in additional resources from Washington, D.C., to help them follow up on the leads they had received. Eventually, twenty federal agents would be involved, hoping to detect a pattern. But if the crimes didn't involve the mail, they were somebody else's problem.

Take Harry Swisher. Presumably, he wasn't Italian. Along with his brother E.W. Swisher of Columbus, he was a millionaire cigar manufacturer in Newark, Ohio, with facilities in Ironton and Portsmouth as well. In May, he was threatened with death and destruction of his home unless he complied with the demands of Black Handers and deposited $1,000 in a pile of railroad ties in the Baltimore & Ohio yard. "He did so, and with two officers secreted nearby, awaited developments."[263] Two automobiles approached the area but then drove off—the package went unclaimed. Afterward, he received another letter, warning him that he would be "Blown to Hell" and that "Revenge is Sweet."[264] Nothing more came of it.

Arthur Ketterling wasn't Italian either. But the mutilated body of the Miami University student was found on May 12, 1909, on the railroad tracks near Oxford, Ohio. At the coroner's inquest, evidence was introduced that suggested Ketterling had been murdered because he had not kept the oath of some secret society to which he belonged. Initially, it was thought he had slashed his own wrists and throat and then jumped in front of a train. However, his brother produced a letter that his mother received after his death which said that Ketterling had been a member of the Black Hand and betrayed the organization's secrets to the police. His mother was likewise warned to "close her mouth."[265] Although the brother doubted it was true, Coroner Burnett ruled it was murder.

However, Salvatore Rizzo (or Rizzio) was Italian. Just after the first of the year, Rizzo, a fifty-one-year-old Cincinnati fruit dealer, had received a letter from Marion, Ohio, demanding that he go to Pittsburgh, Pennsylvania, and pay $5,000 in tribute. Rizzo was instructed to walk across a bridge spanning the Allegheny River at midnight on a designated date. He was to carry the money in one hand and, in the other, a live chicken. A man would meet him there and take the money but leave the chicken behind. Presumably, the chicken was to ensure he wasn't carrying a weapon.

A second letter followed, this one from Chicago, telling Rizzo to heed the warning and send the money. A few days after that, a third arrived from a small town in South Dakota, stating much the same thing. Except for the chicken, this attempted shakedown of Rizzo had all of the hallmarks of a Society of the Banana, especially the participation of Black Hand members in Cincinnati, Pittsburgh, Marion and South Dakota. However, Rizzo ignored the threats. Then in May 1909, he suddenly experienced throat trouble and died. Although the two doctors who attended him believed he died of natural causes, his family feared he had been poisoned.

While Black Hand vengeance continued to be very much on the minds of the Italian immigrants who felt powerless to do anything about it, William Baker, New York's new police commissioner (Bingham was fired after the Petrosino murder) quietly disbanded the Italian squad. He purportedly was unwilling to risk any more high-profile deaths. Baker would soon resign as well, accused of interfering in gambling investigations.

# 14
# DAY OF RECKONING

*We have absolute evidence that a division meeting of the black hand was held at Bellefontaine, Ohio, a few weeks ago and immediately thereafter the members of the gang who had voted on the division of the spoils sent $2,000 in postal money orders to Italy from the post office at Marion.*[266]
*—Abraham R. Holmes*

F ive months after someone left a bomb on John Amicon's doorstep, a general conference of postal inspectors was convened in Columbus. On Monday, June 7, 1909, Inspector Frank Oldfield assembled his men in Postmaster Harry Krumm's office to review the battle plan for the next day. He was acting on orders from Inspector-in-Charge Abraham R. Holmes, who had remained in Cincinnati. As agents of the U.S. Postal Inspection Service, they were empowered to carry firearms, serve warrants and make arrests anywhere in the country.[267] At the meeting's conclusion, the inspectors quietly set out for a handful of towns scattered across Ohio.

Early Tuesday morning, Oldfield strolled into Salvatore "Sam" Lima's fruit store on North Main Street in Marion, followed by Inspectors E.F. Hutches and R.M.C. Hosford.[268] It was the site of earlier surveillance. As relatives and employees fumed, Lima and Joe Rizzo were placed under arrest. However, they soon regained their composure and even offered to assist the officers with their search of the premises. Two other suspects—Sebastiano Lima and Antonio Lima, Sam's brother and father, respectively—were

**HARRY W. KRUMM**
Postmaster

Postmaster Harry W. Krumm of Columbus was mad about automobiles. *Authors' collection.*

nowhere to be found. In all, four Rizzos would be arrested before they got the one they wanted.

Quoting postal officials, the *Marion Daily Mirror* reported, "Marion is the headquarters of a band of 'Black Hand' workers, who have been using the mails to send threatening letters to intended victims, promising dire vengeance if the society's demands are not complied with."[269] While rummaging through the store, the investigators uncovered a large bundle of letters, which they believed contained correspondence with many of the gang's victims. There was little evidence to suggest that either Lima or Rizzo were the actual ringleaders, so suspicion fell on two other Marion residents—Sebastiano and Antonio Lima.

Sam Lima was taken to the city prison while Joe Rizzo was confined in the county jail. Both men were watched closely. As the hours passed, hundreds of Italians gathered in the streets, and the authorities became worried that an attempt would be made to free them. That evening, the inspectors picked up two more suspects, Salvatore Z. "Sam" Rizzo (not to be confused with the Cincinnati fruit dealer of the same name) and Joe Batagalia (sometimes Bataglia, Battaglia, Batazlio or Botella), as they were attempting to skip town. They were located in a rooming house directly across the street from Lima's store.

It wasn't until the next morning that Sam Lima learned the reason for his arrest. Handed a newspaper, he was surprised to read that he was suspected of being behind the plot to blackmail Amicon. "Amicon is jealous," Lima ranted. "That is all. He is jealous of me because I sell more bananas in Ohio that he does."[270] A guard was posted at the jail and the militia placed on alert; the prisoners awaited the arrival of a United States marshal who would take them to Toledo for trial.

Puffing away on a cigar while fielding questions from his cell, Lima was described as a rather docile prisoner. However, his temper would flare at any mention of the Black Hand. When asked if he had any connection to such an organization, he leaped to his feet and began gesticulating wildly. "See, my hands are white. They are not black. I am a hard working businessman. I work every day, every night and every Sunday."[271] It was observed that he could not straighten his arm because of a poorly mended break at the elbow. A married father of two, Lima told reporters he had lived in Marion for three years. He maintained that he, his father and two brothers were all innocent. In contrast, Rizzo was sullen and not interested in talking to anyone.

At 7:15 that evening, the inspectors left Marion on the Hocking Valley Railroad. Arriving in Columbus at midnight, they went to the home of fruit dealer Savario Ventola, 326 East Spring Street, accompanied by Detectives Richard Owens and William Nugent. Ventola had been in competition with the Amicons for at least a decade. The inspectors were expecting to find documents connecting him with the attempt to extort money from the brothers. According to John Amicon, Ventola had paid a visit to him several weeks earlier and asked him not to press charges. Since he had not discussed the extortion attempt with him, Amicon "was puzzled to know how Ventola knew of the conditions unless he was in confidence with the black handers."[272]

Although the inspectors found no evidence to arrest Ventola, one Tony Bicherio was taken into custody. Since no further mention was made of him, either the name was wrong or he was soon released. About the same time, more than one hundred miles to the east of Marion, Antonio Vicarrio was apprehended in Dennison, a village in Tuscarawas County, halfway between Columbus and Pittsburgh. Taken to Canton, Vicarrio was charged with using the mail with intent to defraud and given a hearing before U.S. Commissioner Julius Whiting on Wednesday. He pleaded not guilty. Unable to post bond, Vicarrio remained in jail.

William Lord Wright, a Bellefontaine native and reporter for the local newspaper, participated in the capture of Collogero "Charles" Vicarrio, one of the wiliest of the gang members.[273] However, for some reason, Wright changed certain names. His firsthand account begins with the arrival of Frank De Farano (this would be Joseph DeMar), who had come to Bellefontaine from Italy to join "a small fruit firm"—obviously Salvatore Cira & Company.

Not long afterward, Joseph DeMar was found murdered. "Salvatore Dirra, a member of the firm, was loud in his protests that he would avenge the sudden death of his young cousin, but he, too, was shot down a few months later in the fruit store by John Dirra, a nephew."[274] Salvatore Dirra was, in fact, Salvatore Cira, and John Dirra was Charles DeMar.

Wright reported that DeMar "told the police that his uncle had rushed at him with a stiletto, and that he had fired in self-defense."[275] The grand jury apparently believed him, and he was acquitted of Cira's death. Following the death of Joseph DeMar, Collogero Niccariotic came to Bellefontaine. Formerly a resident of Marion (and/or Cleveland), he settled into a job as a clerk/partner in the DeMar & Company fruit business. "He stated that he was engaged to marry a girl in sunny Italy, and that the ceremony was only delayed while he saved some money with which to start housekeeping."[276]

An artist's conception of the capture of Collogero Vicarrio in Bellefontaine. *Authors' collection.*

Niccariotic was, clearly Vicarrio (aka Diedario or Diodardio). In a copy of a telegram published with the article, Niccariotic is referred to as "Viccario," but Wright wrote that it was a mistake. "His real name was then, and still is, unknown to the Italian or American Secret Police"—which may be true of some of the other suspects as well.[277]

On the evening of June 8, as "thunder crashed" and "rain fell in torrents," Police Chief Edward L. Faulder met with a group of newspaper reporters at the Bellefontaine jail.[278] Someone had leaked that the U.S. Secret Service (i.e., postal inspectors) was in town to investigate the Black Hand activities. Faulder introduced the reporters to Inspectors Hosford and "Charles Tate" (presumably George Pate). "Before morning we expect to capture an Italian criminal long sought for by the Government," he told them. "This man and his confederates are shrewd and desperate....If you are willing to take the risk you can accompany us on this raid."[279] They asserted that Collogero

"Charles" Vicarrio, the quiet Italian clerk, was a criminal of international reputation.[280] They even dubbed him the "King of Black-Handers" and linked him to the murder of Lieutenant Petrosino.[281]

At about three o'clock in the morning on Wednesday, June 9, during the height of the storm, they made their way to the southwestern outskirts of Bellefontaine. Faulder and the inspectors approached the door of a "rude cabin" while other officers trained their guns on the windows, ready "to open fire upon the slightest provocation."[282] The cabin was the home of Mary D. Cira, widow of Salvatore Cira, and the scene of his murder. Mary took in boarders, mostly DeMars (her own family) and Vicarrios. In fact, Collogero was planning to marry her fourteen-year-old daughter, also named Mary or Maria.

When Faulder pounded on the door with the butt of his gun, he was answered by the barking of dogs. Someone slowly opened the door and the officers rushed in, beating back the dogs with their weapons. Niccariotic/Vicarrio was surprised in his bed. "With a snarl of rage the man reached for a shot-gun which lay under the bed," Wright wrote. "Before he could grab it, however, he faced the muzzles of three revolvers and sullenly surrendered."[283]

Not only was Vicarrio heavily armed and carrying $1,000 in cash, but the women and children in the house—likely Mary's teenage daughters—were armed as well. Three sawed-off shotguns, a number of pistols, daggers and knives were seized, as well as a large tin can filled with gold and silver coins. According to Inspector Oldfield, a trunk found in Vicarrio's room contained an abundance of Black Hand literature. Taken to Toledo by Marshal Chandler, Vicarrio was "charged with being the go between in securing money for the Black Hand gang that has been run down at Marion and Columbus."[284]

Like Sam Lima, Vicarrio had a crippled arm. He had sustained a broken right shoulder and was unable to raise his arm to full height. For some reason, he was suspected to have been involved in the murder of Salvatore Cira two years earlier and even to have been the triggerman (rather than in conjunction with Charles DeMar). While the subject of Vicarrio's release on a writ of habeas corpus was being argued in court, Chief Faulder had his men transport the prisoner to the Ohio Penitentiary, which at the time also held federal prisoners. Told that a confederate had already confessed, Collogero Vicarrio would only curse and say nothing. According to the *New York Times*, "He went to Bellefontaine from Cleveland two years ago, and is originally from Messina, where, it is said, he lost his mother and brother in the earthquake."[285]

Also on Wednesday morning, Augustino "Gus" Marfisi, age forty-three, was arrested in Dennison following a running gun battle with deputies and Secret Service agents. Marfisi was Antonio Vicarrio's employer. The investigators noted that Marfisi had been in Italy when Barney Boneti (aka Billy Bandana), a Dennison fruit dealer, was murdered. Boneti had sold his store and fled to Italy to escape Black Hand threats. Soon after Boneti's death, Marfisi returned home. Authorities strongly suspected he was involved. Tipped off that a mob of Italians planned to storm the Dennison jail in an effort to free Marfisi, extra deputies were hastily sworn in. They guarded the structure until the prisoner was driven to Canton the next day for arraignment before Commissioner Whiting. Meanwhile, Inspector Hutches had been dispatched to Cleveland, where he apprehended brothers Giuseppe and Giacemo (or Antonio and Sebastian) Nuzzo, suspecting them of being members of the Marion gang.[286]

In the Marion raid, Pinkerton Detective Dimaio oversaw the collection of evidence. Inspector Oldfield had quickly returned to Columbus with two bags of mail removed from Lima's residence, located in apartments above the store. A trunk full of letters written in Italian confiscated from Vicarrio was shipped to Columbus as well. Oldfield reviewed them all with Postmaster Krumm. Krumm had risen from "a little, ragged, hustling news urchin of the streets" to postmaster of Columbus, a city of 200,000.[287] With a budget approaching $700,000 and a salary of $6,000, he had nearly 300 people in his employ. He was known for his passion for fast automobiles, having already owned by 1900 "nearly a half dozen."[288]

Wednesday afternoon, Deputy U.S. Marshals Amos F. Owens and B.J. Wagner arrived in Marion with warrants for the prisoners, sworn out by Hutches. They charged Sam Lima, Salvatore Rizzo and Joe Batagalia with devising a scheme to extort money from John Amicon. The threatening letters, written in Italian, had been forwarded to Marfisi at Dennison with instructions to mail them to Amicon. The marshals left with their prisoners at 4:20 in the afternoon for Toledo, where a preliminary hearing would take place before U.S. Commissioner Frederick W. Gaines.

The same afternoon, Oldfield had Savario Ventola brought to the postmaster's office, where he questioned him for more than an hour. No doubt the fact that Ventola had served a prison term fifteen years earlier cast him as a prime suspect. However, he did not admit to anything, asserting he would never say a word even if he were tried for a thousand years. Then late Wednesday night, Inspector Oldfield, accompanied by Chief Deputy U.S. Marshal T.J. Howe, placed Ventola under arrest. While sorting through the

Collogero Vicarrio (handcuffed) arriving in Cincinnati with Inspector Oldfield, while Sam Lima and his family stand in front of his Marion store. *Authors' collection.*

bags of mail, Oldfield discovered one of the letters Ventola had written to Marfisi warned him "not to send the 'merchandise' to Columbus at this time because it was very 'hot' there."[289] Salvatore Lima had been the recipient of a similar letter.

All of the letters were described as being Black Hand, written in the same hand with the same ink and on the same paper (it had a "Buckeye" watermark). The letters implicated at least half a dozen other men in the scheme. They reinforced the belief that Marion was the headquarters of the gang and that Sam Lima was the leader. Hundreds of other men were believed to have been affiliated with the gang in some manner.

Following the initial wave of raids, the investigators continued to pursue the gang members who had eluded them, particularly Antonio Lima. Suspected of being a leader, he was soon traced to Upper Sandusky but then disappeared, presumably having returned to Italy. Hidden from an attorney and interrogated for three hours, Collogero Vicarrio revealed nothing that would help them. Meanwhile, two interpreters—a man and a woman—were kept occupied all day Friday translating the confiscated letters.

Chief Inspector Holmes described the circuitous route traveled by the extortion letters on their way to the victims. Someone in Cincinnati might be selected as a victim. He would likely receive a first letter from Marion, demanding money on pain of death. A second letter, written by the same person, would be sent from Pittsburgh. If the victim still did not pay tribute, a third letter, also in the same handwriting, would come to him from Chicago.

According to Holmes, they had obtained evidence that as recently as two weeks earlier members of the group had sent post office money orders from Marion to Italy in the amount of $1,900, representing a division of the profits with confederates located there. And the total may have actually been $3,000.[290] (The Society had kept careful accounts of the division of the spoils.) "The proof we have found against the gang convinces us that they have worked their game successfully on many Italians, principally well-to-do Sicilians," said Holmes. "We have not found where they threatened any American. If their demands were ignored they resorted to the bomb to bring their victim time."[291]

Evidence suggested that, at Sam Lima's direction, gang members from all over Ohio and western Pennsylvania would convene in Marion, where they provided updates on the targeted victims. When the victims refused to pay, options were discussed, with the final decision being left up to Lima. He would also assign certain members to carry out the vengeance. While it was not thought that Lima led a national organization, it was felt that he had control of a certain portion of the country and had been in communication with other leaders both in the United States and Italy.

Holmes said his men discovered evidence that Marion was the "headquarters of all the Black Hand societies of the country, and they allege that Lima is the head of the organization."[292] The safe in Lima's store contained "evidence that hundreds of business men in all parts of the State and country had been paying tribute to the gang."[293] The seized letters had been received from points as far west as South Dakota. The postal inspectors asserted, "The handwriting is identical with that in letters received by Antonio Rizzo, of Cincinnati, who died suddenly after refusing to pay $1,000."[294] Rizzo fell ill after eating a banana given him by a stranger to sample. Before his burial, an attempt was made to set fire to his coffin. The writing also matched that of a letter received by Joseph Ammarino (or Annarino) of Cincinnati, who was warned his child would be kidnapped if he didn't pay $10,000.

The investigators learned that there were three "degrees" in the Black Hand Society. The lowest degree was the Garzone di Mala Vita (lad of bad life).[295] He was the new recruit who had yet to prove himself. The next highest was the Picciotto di Sgarro (boy who avenges every slight).[296] He had been voted into the group but was still at the beck and call of those who outrank him. And the third was the Camorrista (racketeer). This was the level from which the Capo (leader) was chosen. Oldfield and his men believed that their first seven arrests were from the third degree.

"Hundreds of others are affiliated with Lima in this particular gang," the *Marion Daily Mirror* reported. "Other societies are also affiliated and are known to have loaned men for certain deeds the society wanted performed."[297] The postal inspectors believed that the numerous knife fights among Italians in Marion were somehow connected to the gang's operations, as was the unavenged murder of Louis Giofritta.

Echoing the opinion of Inspector Oldfield, the *New York Times* observed that while the New York police doubted the existence of a large Black Hand organization, the work of the Cincinnati officers seemed to show they were wrong. Not only was there a national organization, "but...it is directly allied with a similar organization in Sicily and is working in connection with the Mafia or 'Order of the Banana,' as it has more recently been known in this country."[298]

On Thursday, June 10, a letter demanding $25,000 was delivered to John Amicon. According to his office manager R. Herman Holland, "We paid no attention to it because it was evidently written by a child who was trying to act funny."[299] In the aftermath of the arrests, Amicon boasted that he was not afraid because he could "fix them" if they "tried any dirty work" with him. "Others have coughed up and have lived in fear. I have kept my money and fells as safe as anyone could. I knew that the arrests would be made and know of others to be made and let me tell you that there will be big doings when they start in to raid all the Black Handers."[300]

## 15

# I'D DIE FIRST

[T]*he Society of the Banana was just a continuation*
*of the old Mafia under a new name.*[301]
—*Frank Dimaio*

obert Storaci, confectioner and respected member of the community,
was not surprised by the Marion raid. Many of his countrymen were
afraid to be prosperous or accumulate wealth, he said, because they
knew they would be preyed upon by those who had no inclination to
work. In his opinion, "The only method of stamping out the Black Hand
in America is by stopping immigration from Italy and the enactment of
stricter laws, making either life imprisonment or death the penalty in case
of conviction."[302]

Following an all-night conference, Inspector Oldfield and Postmaster
Krumm decided to dispatch agents to Springfield, Ohio, as well. They had
turned up a clue that some Black Hand operations might have been directed
from that city, fifty miles west of Columbus. So the next day, Thursday, June
10, Inspectors Pate and Hosford hopped an early morning train with orders
to track down two more suspects. They apparently did not find them.

Escorted to Columbus, Collogero Vicarrio was rearrested by federal
authorities on Thursday afternoon when he stepped off the train. Meanwhile,
Sam Lima returned to Marion after he was released on $3,000 bond in
Toledo, while Savario Ventola was freed on $5,000 bond in Columbus.[303]
Lima and Ventola were regarded as the "craftiest men" in the organization.[304]

Crowds thronged the streets of Bellefontaine in the aftermath of the bombing. *Authors' collection.*

Joe Rizzo, Salvatore Rizzo and Joe Batagalia were also quietly released when it was determined they had no involvement in the conspiracies, while in Dennison an extra guard had been posted around the jail to thwart any attempt to spring Augustino Marfisi. Three other members of the Black Hand remained at large.

From the onset, John and Charles Amicon had been the prime targets of the Society of the Banana. The wealthy brothers operated two large commission houses in Columbus and six branches in other towns, including one in Marion in direct competition with Lima. When asked to comment on the attempt to blackmail him, John Amicon was especially defiant. "They got hold of the wrong fish," he said. "I'm not afraid of any man in the United States. I wouldn't pay a cent. I'd die first. I've turned every letter over to the postmaster as soon as it came. They might kill me, but I would never pay."[305]

Frank Macusia (or Macuala), who operated a fruit stand in Central Market, paid an initial $500 and then was forced to pay another $500 because he talked too much. Frank Lascola, another Central Market fruit vendor, admitting paying $200. Charles Ferraro, the owner of an Italian grocery in St. Paul, Minnesota, was relieved to hear of the arrest of the Black Hand members in Ohio. He said he had received a telegram from them two weeks earlier, demanding a loan of $5,000—which, if so, marked a curious change in their typical method of operation.

After an eight-month-long investigation by twenty agents, Inspector Hosford was claiming that they had uncovered a nationwide operation "with the more important branches in New York, Chicago, Philadelphia, and Pittsburg. The little Ohio towns of Marion and Bellefontaine were used as a general clearing house. The New York office handled the blackmailing business of the East, and the Chicago branch was the centre of operations on the Pacific Coast."[306]

In the days that followed, postal authorities continued to search for evidence that would support their belief (more of a hope) that they had broken the back of the Black Hand. But despite their continued bravado, it was starting to appear that much of their case rested on hyperbole rather than actual fact.

Between one and three o'clock on the morning of Saturday, June 12, four days after the first Marion raid, burglars broke into John Amicon's office by prying the lock off the rear door with a crowbar. They ransacked the safe, which was customarily unlocked, as well as some drawers. All they got for their efforts were 175 old pennies, a silver dollar, other assorted change and a lady's gold watch. Presumably, they were looking for more.

The postal inspectors were looking for more, too. Just after six o'clock on Saturday evening, Oldfield and Pate, with assistance from the Marion police, raided the home, store and barn of Sam Lima. Having obtained a search warrant in the mayor's court, the inspectors immediately sprang into action. They confiscated two guns, a large quantity of ammunition, several stilettos, a bullet-loading outfit and a large sack full of letters. In Lima's living quarters, the men found a photograph of Sam Lima hidden behind a clock. He was wearing a uniform—believed to be that of an Italian secret order—and had a bullet hole where his heart would have been. The hole matched the caliber of the bullets confiscated.

Free on bail, Lima did not try to obstruct the search but stood in the corner, indignant. However, he was able to delay the authorities' search of the premises until one of the six women present was able to escape. The inspectors suspected she grabbed some documents that would have revealed the whereabouts of Sebastiano Lima. One of the guns confiscated also disappeared, snatched away by Mrs. Lima, who then ran with it out to the barn, where she was thought to have handed it off to a confederate. Although the officers turned the barn upside down, they could not locate the missing weapon.

The ammunition they found was identical with that seized in Dennison, Bellefontaine and other towns raided by the officers. It consisted of 12-gauge shotgun shells loaded with one-ounce slugs, behind which was a load of buckshot. The paper wads on top of the bullets were marked with a cross similar to the ones on the Amicon letters. The two captured guns were short, the barrels about eighteen inches long, so they could easily be concealed under a long coat. Loaded and ready to be used, they matched those taken from the Bellefontaine arsenal. Both the weapons and the ammunition were characteristic of Black Handers. In fact, the inspectors now believed that more than thirty murders committed in Cincinnati, Columbus, Cleveland and Dayton could be traced to the distinctively marked shells and marble-sized bullets used by the Society of the Banana.

Oddly, the *Marion Daily Mirror* reported, "Before the postal inspectors left Columbus Saturday afternoon they gave the information to Columbus newspaper men and the account of the search, what was seized etc., reached this city over the associated press wires, two hours before the search was made."[307] However, the suspects apparently did not know this.

Meanwhile, Sergeant Victor P. Churches was warned that assassination attempts might be made on him. He had played a critical role in interpreting the letters and assisting federal authorities in securing evidence. Someone who knew Churches called the Columbus city prison on Sunday night and said that two strange Italians had been in the city from Pittsburgh and had made threatening remarks. "We will look Churches up and get him," they reportedly told people.[308] They were said to be in town to collect payments from other Italians who had received threatening letters.

On Monday, June 14, Deputy Marshals Amos F. Owens and B.J. Wagner and Inspector Hosford arrived in Marion from Toledo at about seven o'clock in the evening. Joined by Chief of Police Levi Cornwell and Patrolmen McDonough and Bell, they went to the Lima home, expecting to find Sebastiano there. However, a thorough search of the premises confirmed that he was not there. One of his daughters attempted to escape from the house, possibly trying to warn her father that it was under guard. So, concealing themselves in the shadows, the federal officers waited. Four hours later, they caught sight of Sebastiano Lima sneaking around the corner of his house. He was quickly overpowered. Marshall Owens returned to Toledo with the prisoner on the late train. The same night, Joseph Nuzzo's house was raided in Cleveland, and guns and stilettos were found.

When Hutches and Hosford reached Toledo on Tuesday, June 15, Hutches stated, "The evidence turning up in papers seized by the Inspectors makes the case appear more serious every day."[309] No doubt, they hoped to influence the bond amounts being set by U.S. District Attorney William Day. Not only was Sam Lima's bond bumped up to $5,000 but Sebastiano Lima's as well. Along with Joe Batagalia and Salvatore Rizzo, the men were arraigned before U.S. Commissioner Gaines on a charge of conspiracy to defraud by use of the mails. Day announced that he would be meeting with the inspectors in Cleveland toward the end of the week.

In retaliation for Mayor William R. Niven's role in curtailing their activities, the Black Hand turned their terror tactics on him a week later. About three o'clock on the morning of Tuesday, June 15, a bomb was hurled through the front window of the mayor's Bellefontaine home. The resulting explosion wrecked the interior of his residence. The bomb consisted of a glass quart-sized bottle filled with nails and pieces of iron as well as some explosive material. Fortunately, Mayor Niven was not at home at the time. If he had been, he likely would have been sitting up reading close by the window. The curtains, carpets and furniture were all ablaze when the fire department arrived.

Mayor Niven's house in Bellefontaine where the bombing took place. *Authors' collection.*

Although two police officers heard the breaking glass, saw the flames and spotted a man fleeing the scene, they assumed he was going to summon help. Within minutes of the fire being extinguished, Mayor Niven was there. He had been elected on a (Prohibition) platform two years earlier and had set about enforcing the city's "dry laws." He also had issued the warrant for the arrest of alleged Black Handers. In a statement to the press, Niven said, "It must have been some one dissatisfied with the way our laws are enforced here. It was not a crime committed on the impulse of the moment, but one carefully and deliberately planned. It was cowardly. I am on the street every day and anybody looking for me could find me without trying to destroy my relatives sleeping at home."[310] However, he was reluctant to blame the Black Hand.

Some days prior to the firebombing, a leaden container was found by a delivery boy in the gutter in front of Niven's home. When the mayor examined it, he discovered it was filled with explosives and took it to police headquarters. Niven admitted that he had received—and disregarded—several Black Hand letters. The bomb throwers left footprints, small with high Cuban heels, in Niven's front yard, so bloodhounds were put on the trail. A local shoe dealer identified the prints as matching some footgear sold to an Italian. The police believed that "the foreign element" was angered by the mayor's order to close fruit stores on Sundays, coupled with the arrest of Charles Vicarrio.[311]

At the close of a conference of postal inspectors in June 1909, U.S. Attorney William Day stated, "I believe that we have the right men, and that through them we may be able to break up the so-called Black Hand Society which has been preying upon wealthy Italians in the Central States."[312] The evidence was compelling. During the past two years, the Society of the Banana had demanded not less than $200,000 from every Italian of means in Pittsburgh, Cincinnati, St. Louis and Chicago. Day became convinced after the first ten arrests that there was an actual organization, something law enforcement had previously denied. And it was based in humble Marion, Ohio.

On the night of Thursday, June 17, nine days after the initial raid in Marion, Francesco Spadera (or Spadero), saloonkeeper, and Vincenzo "Vincent" Arrigo, fruit dealer, were arrested in Cincinnati by Oldfield and his deputies and held as leaders of the Society of the Banana.[313] The *New York Times* reported, "Recently, they had changed their name from Society of the Banana to Society of the Brothers of Law. Spadera was made leader and Salvatore Lima of Marion was elected superintendent."[314] A bloody stiletto was among the weapons confiscated.

The arrests were tied to those made earlier in Marion, Columbus and other Ohio towns. All were, as the *New York Times* pointed out, "foreigners."[315] As soon as Salvatore Arrigo heard that his son and eleven other men in the house on Sixth Street had been jailed, he disappeared. During the course of his investigation, Inspector Oldfield discovered what he believed was a connection between the Arrigo-Spadera mob and two other unsolved assassinations that had shocked the country: those of Joe Petrosino and David Hennessy. What they had in common was Collogero "Charles" Vicarrio (aka Diedario), now the main suspect in the killing of Salvatore Cira in Bellefontaine.

At eleven o'clock on Saturday night, June 19, postal inspectors, Pinkertons and Pittsburgh detectives took Orazio Runfola (aka Orozer Rumfalo and other names)—"the Pittsburgh end of the alleged Black Hand society"—into custody near his home at 2210 Penn Avenue.[316] They had been shadowing him for several days. Aiding Postal Inspector George V. Craigshead and Pinkerton Detective Dimaio, who had been stationed in the post office, were Detectives Dackroth and McDonough. Craigshead followed Runfola as he left the post office and intercepted him as he was opposite the police station. At first, Runfola tried to throw the letters away; failing that, he tried to eat them, but the police already knew their contents.

Many of the letters had been sent to Runfola from Black Hand leaders in Ohio who had been arrested. He had in his possession many other letters from the likes of Salvatore and Sebastiano Lima (Marion), Savario Ventola (Columbus), Augustino Marfisi and Antonio Vicarrio (Dennison), Francesco Spadera and Salvatore Arrigo (Cincinnati), and Antonio Nuzzo (Cleveland). Following his apprehension, it was "alleged that Rumfalo [sic] has been the brains of the Black Hand troubles in Ohio and [had] written most of the threatening letters."[317]

Shortly after one o'clock in the morning on Sunday, Giuseppe "Peppino" Galbo was arrested by postal inspectors who swooped down on his fruit store in Meadville, Pennsylvania. Galbo, who was believed to be working for Runfola, was the fifteenth man arrested in the ongoing crusade against the Society of the Banana. Born in Sicily on July 26, 1872, Galbo came to the United States in 1899 at the age of twenty-seven. Ten years later, he joined the Society of the Banana at the invitation of Sam Lima, or so he said. In 1905, Galbo moved to Meadville from Buffalo, New York. Since then, he had acquired nearly $10,000 in property. During the raid, a large quantity of letters and other paperwork were found in Galbo's room.

When Runfola was told that it had been rumored that he squealed after his arrest, setting the law officers on the trail of Galbo, he begged the police to deny it. "They will murder me. They will kill me for sure," he said, paralyzed with fright. "They will kill me when I get out."[318] Both men were alleged to be Pennsylvania agents of the Society of the Banana who "used Galbo's store in Meadville as a clearing house for Black Hand operations in [that] section."[319] They were subsequently charged with mailing a letter from the Pittsburgh post office to "Ciali" (Charles) Amicone at 3 North Grant Street in Columbus. It was one of seven Amicon letters.

*Dearest Friend, Ciali Amicone:*

*Last week our band at Pittsburgh, Penn., sent two of us to Columbus, Ohio, and put dynamite behind your door, and behind the door of your brother John, accompanied by two letters in which you were notified by our band to pay $10,000, which for your firm is only a hair of your head. If you refused it is under the penalty of death for you and your children and all the family.*

*Now we will show you the way. If you search for honorable persons, most honorable, giving them money, who will leave Columbus for Pittsburgh. This person arrives in Pittsburgh, Penn., and goes searching for persons, and while he is searching he will be found by us. There must be no more than two persons, and this must be between the first and tenth of February, and if no one presents himself the eleventh he will return to Columbus and pay attention to our orders. Then in case you favor us, you can continue your affairs. You will be peaceful you can get out night and day and no one will molest you for by us you will be protected. In case you refuse, we will give you a taste of our daggers and our trusty carbines, which have never failed, and which cannot fail. We will kill you like a hog.*

*We have decided by lot, and the two chosen must kill you even in the midst of a thousand police. We have killed Kings, Emperors, and Presidents. Consider this was in the midst of thousands and thousands of police. Consider yourself, worm of the earth. Two who will come are obliged to kill, even though they themselves must pay the death penalty. Woe unto you if you turn to the police. We are brigands escaped from Italy, and the police look like flies to us. Take account and discuss it in your family because no one under our hands can free himself. Read the newspapers and see what we have done in New York, Chicago, New Orleans, and Pittsburgh.*

*We advised you that we have dynamite—a double load—that will send your house up in the air and kill all who are within, and we will do the same to your brother. Understand that our band is in the whole world, and were hold all under our feet, especially the police. Woe if you refuse. We have you registered in our register that you must pay the money or your head be brought to Pittsburgh, Penn. For the person who joins our band shall have killed ten men before. Don't get a crazy notion in your head, for you have to deal with men who will eat you raw. Either the money or your life.*

*THE HUMAN BUTCHERS.*[320]

After the arrests of Runfola and Galbo, Oldfield, who had been directing all field operations, and Hutches came to Pittsburgh on June 20. Holing up with Inspector Craighead, they delved into the new evidence that had been uncovered. "The post office inspectors intimated…that they have hopes of giving the case a still more sensational turn, by connecting nearby Italians with the murder in Sicily recently of Detective Petrosino, the New York detective who paid with his life the penalty of running down the Black Hand."[321]

According to Oldfield, the letters found on some of the Ohio prisoners showed that they had regularly sent money orders to Sicily to aid in the defense of the Italians rounded up after Petrosino's murder. Investigators ransacked Runfola's business and apartments searching for clues. Despite offers from his friends to post his bail, Runfola remained in the Pittsburgh jail, awaiting a hearing before U.S. Commissioner William W. Lindsey. As Oldfield observed, "Government officers are constantly blocked…by Italian victims of the Black Hand. Men forced to pay money to the gang by threats of death, kidnaping of their children or destruction of their property by bomb, are said to be afraid to testify against the society."[322]

16

# BAD ENGLISH

*Had all Italians the courage of John Amicon of this city...the Black Hand would long since have been practically exterminated.*[323]
—*L.H., the* New York Times

espite claims to the contrary, the crackdown on the Society of the Banana did little to stem the flow of Black Hand letters. Other would-be extortionists, some within "a stones' throw of the federal building in Cincinnati," continued to crank them out.[324] Although many laughed at the very name—the Society of the Banana and Faithful Friends—Post Office Inspector Hosford assured the press that "the name is a real one and not, as some supposed, a joke."[325] Both Hosford and Oldfield received threatening letters in the weeks following the arrests of the suspects, warning them they would meet with horrible deaths unless they dropped their plans to prosecute them. John Amicon also received one, this time demanding payment of $25,000.

On July 1, Collogero Vicarrio and Savario Ventola were hauled before U.S. Commissioner A.H. Johnson in Columbus for a preliminary hearing on charges of conspiracy to use the U.S. mails to defraud.[326] Both men were bound over to the grand jury to be tried in Toledo along with other alleged gang members. Creditors of DeMar Fruit Company—the Amicon Brothers, D.W. Askrom of Bellefontaine and the Toledo & Ohio Central Railroad—quickly petitioned to have the company declared bankrupt. They claimed that a large sum of money purportedly stolen from the DeMar Fruit

The federal building in Cincinnati was the site of some preliminary hearings. *Library of Congress.*

Company and owed to them had actually been taken by Vicarrio. He had $640 tucked under his pillow when he was arrested.

The following day, Francesco Spadera, saloonkeeper, and Vincent Arrigo, fruit dealer, were brought before the U.S. commissioner for a hearing on their involvement in Cincinnati's Black Hand Society. Evidence in the possession of government officers showed that the suspects had been meeting regularly in a room in the downtown business district. Eight days later, Inspector Holmes noted that "it had taken five men six months to run the leaders down."[327]

While en route to his home in Athens, Oldfield stopped off in Columbus on Saturday morning, July 3, 1909. Had he picked up the *Cincinnati Enquirer* that morning, he would have noticed that another Amicon letter had been published:

> *You fly. What do we care for you? We will eat your heart if you do not give us the $10,000. We are butchers. We are brigands escaped from Italy. Our*

*carbines are trusty and they will never fail us. We have been sent to kill, even if you had 100 police guarding you. You told the police, did you? We'll get you. Then you will remember your wife and children.*[328]

In his quest not to leave any stone unturned, Oldfield wanted to see for himself if the unfortunate Joe Colluccio had been driven mad due to threats by the Black Hand. Currently held at the county jail on a lunacy charge, he was being treated by Drs. Deschle and Tarbell. Incredibly, they brought in accused Black Hander Collogero Vicarrio to translate for them. But other than turning over all of the blackmail letters he had received to the investigators, Colluccio provided little information of consequence. Nevertheless, when he was released three days later, having been "cured" by his doctors, he planned to return to work, satisfied that the police would protect him from further Black Hand difficulties.

By the third week of July, Sam Lima's fruit store and the apartments in which he lived with his family had been vacated. With their patriarch in jail, the Limas had been unable to continue operating the business. Creditors moved in on them, and they sold out. Mrs. Lima and her children moved into the home of Giuseppe "Joe" Ignoffo on Leader Street in Marion. "Since the Black Hand raids here, the Italians in Marion have caused little or no trouble for the police, where they were the cause of much worry," the *Marion Daily Mirror* reported.[329]

Mrs. Lima continued to argue that her husband was innocent, that he was a hardworking man who got up at four o'clock in the morning and worked until late at night, all year around. "He sent money to Italy, of course, and often, too. But he sent it for his fellow countrymen who had given him their savings to forward to Italian relatives. Many times he did this."[330] She was not alone in her opinion. Many who knew Lima and the other suspects found it hard to believe that they were guilty of the crimes with which they were charged. While there was disagreement on whether Lima could have been the leader of any group, they all agreed that he would have had little time to devote to Black Hand operations.

Some known members of the Society of the Banana still remained on the loose. On the night of Friday, July 23, Inspector Oldfield, along with Inspector George Pate and Deputy U.S. Marshal W.J. Sanderson, trailed Salvatore Arrigo to a remote cabin one and a half miles from Craver Station in Clermont County, six miles from Batavia. They had been seeking Arrigo ever since June 17, when he purportedly left Cincinnati. Several hours earlier, they had heard that "a strange Italian had been seen in the neighborhood."[331] He was rumored to be the guest of Pasquale Scantallo.

Procuring a vehicle, the men left an hour before sundown for Craver Station. When they arrived, a farmer gave them directions to Scantallo's cabin. As they approached it, they saw a shotgun on the porch. Quietly, they grabbed the gun "and then, opening a door leading from the porch into a sitting room, entered and seized two men who were so completely taken by surprise that they sat helpless in their chairs."[332] Arrigo offered no resistance but refused to talk, stating, "Me no understand bad English."[333] Having succeeded Spadera, Arrigo now bore the title of "Overseer and President of the Society of the Banana" and was charged accordingly.[334]

An unidentified woman bearing a scar on her check inflicted by a lover had inadvertently played a role in Arrigo's capture by mislaying a letter from him. "She did not give any direct clew [sic] regarding his whereabouts, but it was known that the man was in communication with her."[335] Furthermore, Inspector Oldfield said that Arrigo was undone by his dietary preferences. Dissatisfied with the fruits and vegetables available in the area, "He had to have his macaroni and spaghetti every day, and somebody had to take it to him."[336] The inspectors were able to identify and follow that person.

Arraigned before U.S. Commissioner Joseph L. Adler at Cincinnati, sixty-seven-year-old Arrigo was jailed in lieu of $5,000 bond. He had lived in the United States for thirty-three years, having emigrated from Termini Imerese, Palermo, Italy. For two years, he had been a Cincinnati resident; previously, he kept a fruit stand in Washington, D.C. At some point, he had served a sentence at Auburn Penitentiary in New York on a charge of counterfeiting. Following his release, Arrigo was assigned to the "Ohio district"—assuming the United States had, in fact, been divided into districts by some criminal band.

One of the letters authorities confiscated indicated that every member of the Society of the Banana must have killed at least ten men. However, they were particular about how they went about doing so: they were not to be marked in any way above the shoulders. "Not a mark must be visible when the victim for burial is laid out."[337] Anyone who violated this rule would be marked for death himself.

Meanwhile, Post Office Inspector-in-Charge Holmes denied the rumor that Augustino "Gus" Marfisi had jumped bond. What actually happened was he had accompanied his family to New York City, where they boarded a ship for Sicily. However, he then returned to Dennison on July 23. None of the other twelve suspects had made any attempt to flee, either.

An anonymous young girl sells bananas at the produce market in Cincinnati. *Library of Congress.*

Non-Italian police officers were quicker to attribute any crime committed by an Italian to the Black Hand. Italian officers, however, were a little more circumspect. This was the case when at eleven o'clock on the night of July 24, 1909, twenty-two-year-old Pasquale Spino and his sixteen-year-old wife Hazel were killed instantly when their home on Elmere Pike in Columbus was blown to smithereens. The Columbus police quickly concluded they were the victims of either a Black Hand plot or a lover's triangle. Their next-door neighbor, Tony Andrania, was arrested on suspicion.

When Sergeant Albanese was called in, he rejected the Black Hand theory because 1) the extortionists normally do not sign their "work" (a Black Hand cross had been painted on the door); and 2) Pasquale Spino had only been in the United States for eight months and had not had time to accumulate any money. This led Albanese to suspect that a jealous suitor was behind it. Although he released Andrania, Sergeant Churches soon rearrested him after learning that his nephew, Frank Medow, had been rebuffed in his attempt to marry Hazel. The painted cross was an attempt to put the investigators off the scent.

On August 6, Oldfield shared with Postmaster General Frank H. Hitchcock evidence he believed would send eighteen Black Hand members to prison for many years. "Letters were sent to nearly every Italian of means living in Pittsburg, Cincinnati, St. Louis, and Chicago, and those who responded with payments were assessed again and again."[338] The inspector had more than two dozen of them. While the Black Hand was rarely mentioned in the correspondence, the Society of the Banana or a "Bunch of Bananas" appeared frequently.

The *New York Times* reported that Lima had been appointed by the Mano Nera in Sicily and put in charge of a territory from Pittsburgh to Chicago and, occasionally, New York City. As Sam Lima's wife was complaining that persecution by the police had practically forced her out of the fruit business, another letter to Amicon was released to the press:

> *Finally you are deaf, but if you think we are fooling no! Ugly wretch! That you are. You will believe it when you see two or more daggers in their hands which we will plunge into your heart. In that moment you will cry for help, but there will be no remedy. It will be useless. We have put you down in the register of the dead, nasty brute….Do not think that you can free yourself. No! No! No one escapes from under our hands. We have stabbed many in Italy and consider that I who write this had a price of 14,000 lire on my*

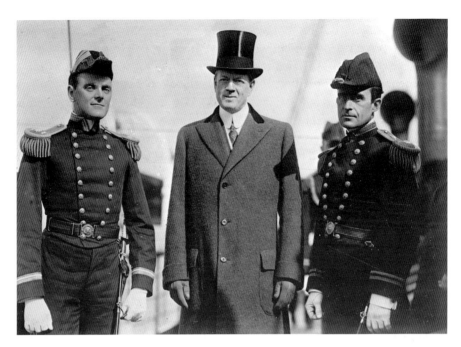

Postmaster General Frank Hitchcock is shown standing between two uniformed officers. *Library of Congress.*

*head and for 8 years was followed by the police and you know not how many I have killed with my trusty carbine, which never failed me.*

*Now we do not wish to have too much idle talk. If the month of February passes and you do not search for one or two persons to come to Pittsburg, Pa., bringing the money and searching and who will be found by us. If you do not obey count yourself as dead. We will come and stab you even if you are in the midst of a thousand police. Your sentence is passed and it cannot be cancelled. Either your blood or your money. If you send the money you will be well respected and we will have you respected over all the world; no one will molest you. Consider well that our hand pardons no one. The black-hand, hand of the devil. Either money or blood. We speak also to your brother.*[339]

It was signed with a cross and the pejorative "Your place, ugly wretch."

Oldfield had tracked the gang's activities to New York City and became convinced that it was connected with the murder of Lieutenant Petrosino. He insisted "that money orders for $3,100 obtained by the band in Cincinnati, [had] been traced, and that the money was undoubtedly used to shield the slayers of Petrosino."[340] Two of the suspects—Augustino Marfisi and Collogero Vicarrio—were known to have been in Palermo on March 12, and they returned to America shortly afterward. While it could have been a coincidence, Oldfield pointed out that "we do know that the gang of which Marfisi is a member is organized exactly like the Society of the Banana today in Sicily."[341] Furthermore, he believed that Vicarrio and Marfisi knew who Petrosino's assassins were and had been sending monthly payments to them. "A letter is alleged to have been found on one of the suspects referring in a graphic manner to a street scene in Sicily that might easily have been the one in which Lieutenant Petrosino was killed."[342]

However, Marfisi claimed that his visit to Italy was a result of his mother and brother having been in the earthquake at Messina, which occurred on December 28, 1908. An estimated 100,000 people died in southern Italy and the island of Sicily. And Vicarrio denied that he was in Sicily at the time. He maintained that he could prove he had been in Bellefontaine or Dennison for the past four years.

The inspectors had intercepted a letter dated March 12, 1909, written by Savario Ventola to Salvatore Lima, the "boss":

> *I believe that Turida told us, who have the establishing, not to make any change. I pray you to see Turida as soon as you get this, and see if he can leave Sunday and got to Bellefontaine as usual, as I and my father are to go see the beef. Turida has a beef to sell, and it would be a favor to me if he would be in Bellefontaine that we could buy it. Our Society of Bananas is composed. I am president here and Cleveland, and the old man Menitta president in Cincinnati. However, in case we must unite, Menitta president over all. I pray you to telephone me and let me know whether Turida will come or not.*[343]

The letter contained nothing threatening but read as though it were addressed to an equal and that Turida might be a superior.

Postal inspectors were dispatched to Bellefontaine at the appointed time. Sam Lima and his father, Antonio Lima, went there as well. They were met by Antonio DeMar, Salvatore DeMar and Charles DeMar. However, no beef was sold—at least no sale was observed by the investigators. Instead, the men went to the DeMar house and remained there all day. On Monday, the Limas purchased nineteen money orders—$100 each—for a total of $1,900, and one for $80, all payable at Trabia, Palermo, Italy, to Camilia Nunzie (or Camilla Nunzi) Ogi A. Lima, a relative. While the inspectors believed the money had been paid by Matteo Rini of Cleveland and several Italians in Cleveland, they all denied it.

Late in May, Savario Ventola and Salvatore Bova of Columbus learned that John Amicon was visiting the post office and suspected an investigation was being initiated. They tried to persuade him to withdraw, but he professed to know nothing about it. A few days later, Ventola wrote Marfisi: "I pray you earnestly if any merchandise arrives, do not send it to Columbus, as the weather is too warm and it will be lost. I received the tobacco and thank you."[344]

Following the coordinated raids in Columbus, Dennison, Marion, Cleveland and Bellefontaine, the task force poured through the many documents it had seized in search of additional clues. The investigators found that fifty-eight letters had demanded close to a quarter of a million dollars. How much they collected was not determined. A typical routing of a letter was as follows: a letter would be sent to Salvatore Lima at Marion and he would forward it to Marfisi at Dennison who mail it to Pittsburgh or take it himself to Orazio Runfola or someone else in the society. Some were sent to Portland, Oregon.

According to the *New York Times*, "The otherwise orderly, industrious and respectable body of Italians who have elected to become citizens of this country" had only themselves to blame for the continued existence of the Black Hand. It was due to "a radical fault in the character of many Italian people—their aversion to denouncing the cutthroats as public enemies."[345] The newspaper noted that the wealthy Italian merchants who received the threats regarded the blackmailers as a private, not public, matter. To inform the police "would be a breach of Italian honor."[346] So when they could not otherwise discourage the predators, they would seek a private means of vengeance.

At noon on Wednesday, December 1, the home of Joe Ignoffo in Marion was searched, and Ignoffo was placed under arrest. Known to be a close friend of Sam Lima, he had been under surveillance for several weeks. The Italian cobbler was taken into custody at his shop by Deputy Marshal Owens, along with Postal Inspectors Oldfield and Pate and Marion police chief Levi Cornwell. In the basement of his home, the officers discovered two shotguns, a revolver, a target rifle and a large quantity of ammunition. The shotguns were loaded with shells that contained a ball the size of a marble. However, the most important find was a stash of letters concealed in an old trunk buried beneath a pile of rubbish.

A married father of three, thirty-five-year-old Ignoffo was considered a hard worker, but he had little to show for it. He and his family had been living hand to mouth, and his arrest would leave them destitute. Interviewed by a reporter for the *Marion Daily Mirror*, Ignoffo asserted that his wife was "dangerously ill."[347] Married to Sam Lima's sister, he had been in the United States for fifteen years. "I never done nothing and I don't see why they take me away from my family," he sobbed.[348]

Following Ignoffo's arrest, the investigators drove back to Columbus. Rumor was they had their sights set on one more suspect. Savario Ventola, a Columbus fruit dealer who had been originally arrested in June and was later released under $5,000 bail, was rearrested the next day, December 2.

The last of the alleged gang members to be apprehended was Salvatore Demma. A Syrian from Bellefontaine, he was jailed in Columbus on December 4. Postal authorities noted that his brother had been "killed in Bellefontaine three years ago by a member of the Black Hand Society, who was himself killed later by a relative of Demma."[349] His brother went by the name DeMar, and he was related by marriage to the Cira family.

As of December 9, 1909, eighty witnesses had been subpoenaed to appear before the federal grand jury in Toledo. The jury would examine nearly one hundred witnesses and a mountain of correspondence before returning "indictments against sixteen Italians and Sicilians suspected of using the mails to obtain money from their wealthy countrymen by means of threats of torture or death" on December 12, 1909.[350] It was now time for Holmes and Oldfield to show their hand.

17

# THE TRIAL

## WEEK ONE

*If the claims of the Secret Service men are warranted by later developments
it would be interesting to know when the Black-Hand center shifted
from the East to Ohio.*[351]
—Brooklyn Standard Union

C hief Inspector-in-Charge Holmes was confident that he and his men
had constructed an ironclad case against Salvatore "Sam" Lima and
company. He had proof that a well-organized Black Hand Society,
with secret handshakes and passwords, was responsible for numerous
crimes in Pittsburgh, Cincinnati, Cleveland, Chicago, Columbus and
elsewhere in the Midwest. Or so he believed. But at no time did Holmes
intend to prosecute the gang for murder, kidnapping, arson or any other
crimes that did not involve violating postal regulations. As a consequence,
no further mention was made of the thirty murders the Society of the
Banana was alleged to have committed. However, on January 3, 1910, it was
announced that Inspector Holmes was being transferred from Cincinnati to
Spokane, Washington.

The trial of the fourteen indicted Black Hand suspects commenced
two weeks later, on Tuesday, January 18, in Toledo federal court before
the Honorable Robert Walker Tayler.[352] The sixth district judge for the
Northern District of Ohio, Tayler had been appointed on February 1, 1905,
by President Theodore Roosevelt. Born in Youngstown, Ohio, he was a
graduate of Western Reserve College and had practiced law in both Ohio

The trial of the Society of the Banana was held in the federal courthouse in Toledo, Ohio. *Library of Congress.*

and New York. His father, Robert Walker Tayler Sr., had been chosen first comptroller of the U.S. Treasury by President Abraham Lincoln.

A week earlier, John Rosasco had been found dead beside a railroad track in Columbus. While it was believed he had been struck and killed by a passenger train, his family was dubious. The brother of John Amicon's wife, the thirty-nine-year-old Rosasco was a salesman for the family produce company, which required that he report to work in the early hours of the morning. His body was discovered before daylight and bore few injuries except about the head. This led some to suggest he had been bludgeoned to death and then placed along the Big Four tracks to make it appear that he had been hit by a locomotive.

It was unlikely, the *Columbus Press-Post* reasoned, that anyone would attack the Amicons, since they were known to be well guarded. However, it was "quite probable that they would select some member of the family, whose habits or daily movements would furnish ample opportunity for such an attack."[353] Nevertheless, the Railroad Commission of Ohio tallied many such fatalities in a given year and categorized Rosasco as a "trespasser" on railroad property.

The impact of Rosasco's suspicious death on the Amicons and the other scheduled witnesses can only be conjectured, but the trial moved ahead as planned. Assigned to argue the prosecution's case was William L. Day, son of a U.S. Supreme Court justice. He was aided by Assistant District Attorney Thomas H. Gary. Over the course of the next ten days, District Attorney Day and his team would present evidence of the actual attempted victimization of fourteen Italians living in Ohio and Indiana. In four instances, they would show that payments had been made to the Society of the Banana. Unfortunately, the other victims had destroyed the letters.

On Tuesday morning, the jury was impaneled and their names subsequently published in the newspapers: William Axe, St. Marys; Henry C. Baltzell, Tiffin; John A. Daour, Piqua; Charles Ghan, Kingsway; John P. Holland, Metamora; Edward A. Kirk, Toledo; Marion Kirk, Montpelier; Thomas J. Lee, Wharton; J.W. Riley, Celina; Elias Sumner, Toledo; Martin C. Trout, Toledo; and John Bird, Bluffton.

After lunch, Attorney Gary began to outline the government's case. He was followed by the attorneys for the defense, beginning with John H. O'Leary, whose clients were Salvatore and Sebastiano Lima, Giuseppe Ignoffo and Salvatore Rizzo. (O'Leary, who had secured Joseph Batagalia's release, planned to argue that the Black Hand Society was a myth.) Although they would represent their own clients as the occasion arose, O'Leary and his associates planned to hold conferences at the end of each day to plan a general line of defense. O'Leary began by insisting there was no conspiracy and that the letters were simply written in the course of conducting legitimate business.

Charles F. Williams then spoke on behalf of Francesco Spadera, Vincent Arrigo and Salvatore Arrigo. He claimed that his clients did not know the other defendants and were simply Cincinnati fruit merchants with good reputations. Jay P. Dawley asked the jury to simply remember his client, Augustino Marfisi, whom he described as a successful Dennison merchant who had no reason to resort to extortion to make a living. Judge Duncan Dow made similar denials for Collogero and Antonio Vicarrio; Augustine F. Connolly for Severio Ventola; John J. Sullivan for Pippino Galbo; and James A. Allen for Salvatore Demma. They were, they claimed, all innocent.

The following day, Frank Oldfield, described as the government's star witness, took the stand. He spent the morning identifying documents ("letters, money-orders, checks, writing papers, memorandum books, and newspaper clippings") and weapons ("short-barreled shotguns, revolvers, dirks, and loaded shells") seized by the inspectors.[354] He also identified each

Postal Inspect J. Frank Oldfield emerged as the star prosecution witness for the government. *Library of Congress.*

of the defendants as he recounted the steps of the investigation and the roles they played in the conspiracy.

The postal inspector described how a letter sent to a victim, Mateo Rini of Cleveland, was first posted in Columbus to Augustino Marfisi in Dennison.

Antonio Vicarrio, Marfisi's clerk, then picked it up at the post office and mailed it to Rini in Cleveland. Postmaster D.C. Mahon of Dennison testified that he had marked twenty-five stamps with a dot of red ink on the letter "O" in the word "Two" and sold them exclusively to Augustino Mafisi and the two Vicarrios. One of these stamps was subsequently used to mail a threatening letter to Rini.

After he traced the letters back to Marion, Oldfield then went there to observe a meeting of Antonio Lima, Salvatore Lima, Giuseppe Ignoffo, Savario Ventola, Salvatore Rizzo and Salvatore Demma on March 9, 1909. At that point, he and his team of investigators had collected enough evidence to place the Limas under arrest. In a raid on Lima's store and residence, they found record books, letters, telegrams and money orders that connected the other defendants with an apparent conspiracy. From a review of these documents, they concluded that there was a criminal organization based in Marion and Salvatore Lima was its head.

With respect to the Amicon case, Oldfield testified he had frequently seen Salvatore Lima, Savario Ventola and Salvatore Demma (aka DeMar) in the vicinity of Amicon's store and fruit yard not long after the Amicons received a threatening letter. He then removed a fulminating cap for a dynamite fuse from his vest pocket and said he had discovered it in an iron box in Lima's home.

Inspector E.F. Hutches was then called to the stand. He described how he had "disarmed Sam Lima as the latter was trying to escape through a window when the officers called to arrest him."[355] Under cross-examination, he admitted he did not know for a fact that a meeting was taking place at Lima's store, only that the men entering the building were not ordinary customers. He personally saw Antonio Lima, Sam Lima, Salvatore Rizzo, Giuseppe Ignoffo, Vincenzo Arrigo, Francesco Spadera, Salvatore Demma and Orazio Runfola that night. Until fairly recently, Hutches had spent much of the decade designing rural mail routes, so he was fairly new to being a postal inspector.

On Thursday, C.O. McLees, a private detective hired to guard John Amicon's residence, testified that on the night of January 29, 1909, he heard someone open the back gate and sneak up toward the house while he was concealed in the shadow of the grape arbor.[356] McLees ordered the man, who was illuminated by the street light, to surrender. Instead, the suspect ran toward the alley; the detective fired at him twice, but he escaped. In the courtroom, McLees identified the suspect as Salvatore Rizzo, whom he had previously seen lurking about during the daytime. However, he admitted he could not be absolutely sure. He also identified Orazio Runfola as a man he had spotted loitering at the saloon across the street from Amicon's place.

Chief of Police E.H. Swanson of Valley City, North Dakota, identified a letter found in an Italian bunkhouse on the Northern Pacific Railroad. Chief of Police Edward Faulder and Patrolman Willis Polly of Bellefontaine recounted their involvement in the apprehension of Collogero Vicarrio. When the suspect was caught, Postal Inspector R.M.C. Hosford quoted him as saying "that he knew all about the Black Hand society, and that if he could be assured of government protection he would give his knowledge to the officers."[357] However, Hosford was not authorized to make such an agreement.

Newspaper accounts of what took place in the courtroom on Friday, January 21, were baffling at times, and it is possible that names and incidents were conflated or misreported. For example, a Fabiano Chincola of *Cincinnati* testified that he paid $1,500 at Spadera's saloon to prevent his children from being kidnapped. The father of ten said that the extortionists had demanded $3,000. Later, a Mrs. Fred Chincola of *Columbus* testified that her husband paid $500 in gold when the Black Hand threatened to blow up their house. Since the original report was that Fred Cianciolo (or Ciancela) of Cincinnati had refused to pay $10,000 and his house was blown up, it is possible that these stories were garbled.

Many witnesses bravely told of their encounters with the Black Hand, while others were fearful of saying much of anything. Vincenzo Purpura, a Dayton fruit dealer suffering from rheumatism, had to be helped into the courtroom. When asked to identify Black Hand letters he had received, he declined, stating that he could not read. His son, George, admitted giving Vincenzo Arrigo fifty dollars on one occasion but insisted it was only a gift.

Baptiste Mercurio, another Columbus fruit dealer, had received four threatening letters—each demanding $5,000—mailed from Valley City, North Dakota. Eventually, he paid $800 to Michael Salamona. Francesco and Spinetta Canatta, a married couple from Columbus, said they had received three letters demanding $1,000, $600 and, finally, $400, threatening their home would be bombed. After the last letter, they took $400 to the house of a friend and gave it to an unidentified person. And Agostino Iannarino acknowledged receiving a Black Hand letter in Sicily after fleeing there following the bombing of his home in Columbus. (While he was testifying in Toledo, the Columbus police stationed guards at his home because he had received a number of letters threatening to kidnap his children.)

O.G. Melaragno, managing editor of *La Italiano*, a weekly Italian-language newspaper based in Cleveland, said that he had received a letter in November 1909 signed, "La Mano Nero." He complied with the writer's demand to publish the following:

> *I swear upon the sacred cross that all the people incarcerated in Toledo are innocent. I am the one that is writing the death letters to Amicon that I will kill him. My organization is so strong that we consider those men nothing in the Toledo jail. Please give this letter to the judge when you have printed it.*[358]

Other victims of the Black Hand who testified included Michele Amato, Greenville; Igazione Fazione, Columbus; George Pash, Coshocton; James Fazzione, Coshocton; Ignazio Gentile, Dayton; Baptiste Fazzio, Cincinnati; Mateo Rini, Cleveland; Ventola Jardina, Indianapolis; and Giovanni Anarino, Cincinnati. All were Italian, and few were literate. Judge Tayler then adjourned for the weekend.

18

# THE TRIAL

## WEEK TWO

*Its tools were murder and arson, its aim robbery, its headquarters at Marion, and it was so much of an organization that it had a constitution and by-laws, just like any sedate and well-meaning club.*[359]
—New York Times

As the trial entered its second week, one reporter observed that half of the defendants were named Salvatore, which meant "Savior" in Italian.

When he took the stand on Monday, January 24, Robert J. Pennell, a Marion mail carrier, acknowledged that he had delivered and picked up many letters at Sam Lima's store. "These…were for the most part, addressed to Italians in Dennison, Columbus, Cleveland, and Pittsburg."[360] Between the middle of March and early June 1909, Augustino Marfisi and Orazio Runfola had received many of them. He pointed out one, purportedly written by Salvatore Rizzo, which threatened John Amicon with death and destruction if he did not comply with the demands of the blackmailers.

One of the most recent letters to Amicon found its author in a particularly prolix mood:

> *Dear John Amicon—We have sent you several letters. We have put dynamite behind your door and you are death. Ugly wretch. You need not lament if when you do not expect it, it will cost you your life. Already our band has you down in the register of the dead. We have arrived at the time and already two of us are under obligations to kill you even though you*

## Sample of a Black Hand Letter
## Sent to Charles Amicon

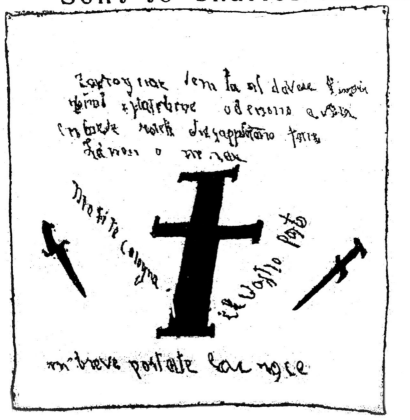

A facsimile of one of the Black Hand letters received by the Amicon brothers. *Authors' collection.*

*are guarded by a thousand police. Take the street as your friend Lieutenant Petrosino did. Ugly wretch that you are, that you content yourself with trying to avoid the payment of the money, $10,000 by the blood of God we are back of you.*

*We have learned your store and you will be accosted when you do not expect it, the sight of two dagger thrusts and then you will sleep forever. One thing I tell you. No one can belong to our band who has not killed 10 persons. We have killed kings and emperors. Consider a fly like you! No! No! Do not think it.*

*We know that you are rich and you must give up some blood. If you wish to avert your death, you will search for an honorable person to come to Pittsburg and while he is searching for us, he will be found. We advise you that if you got to the police, you can count yourself dead—that is, you die first.*

*Wretch! Do your duty without the police and it will be well. Either money or your life! In a short time you will see that we know how to do it. Soon you will bear the cross.*[361]

The letter was signed with a black hand beneath a drawing of a dagger. On either side were the words "Die wretch" and "Your place!"

John Amicon testified he had seen Salvatore and Sebastiano Lima, Savario Ventola, Joe Ignoffo and Salvatore Arrigo loitering in the vicinity of his store during the period in which he was receiving the threatening letters. He said that when Ventola accused him of suspecting him to be the author of the letters, he replied, "If I thought you wrote them, I wouldn't have to go to court. I would shoot you right here on the sidewalk."[362]

The defense team began presenting its case on Tuesday. A total of twenty lawyers were involved, led by John H. O'Leary, who made the opening statement after the court overruled the defense motion to dismiss the case for lack of evidence. The highlight of the day was completely contradictory testimony by two "experts."

William G. Pengelly, a handwriting expert from Columbus with fifteen years' experience, testified that the letters were all written by the same hands, although they had been mailed from different parts of the country.[363] Originally from Plymouth, England, Pengelly had risen from secretary to president of the Capital City Bank. The author of numerous articles on how to safeguard against forgery, he asserted that in his opinion the letter writers were Sam Lima, Pippino Galbo, Charles Vicarrio and Giuseppe Ignoffo.

However, Hialmer Day Gould, an expert in "nerve tremo" theory with more than twenty years' experience, countered that the letters were not written by the same person.[364] A resident of Cleveland, Gould came from Mt. Union College to take a job as a teacher at the Euclid Avenue Business College. In 1901, he testified on behalf of the defense in the late Mae Fleming forgery case in Mansfield, Ohio, insisting that the signatures he examined on a document were genuine, despite the fact that everyone involved denied having signed it.[365]

The accused seemed to have generally been held in high regard in their communities. The defense called a parade of character witnesses to

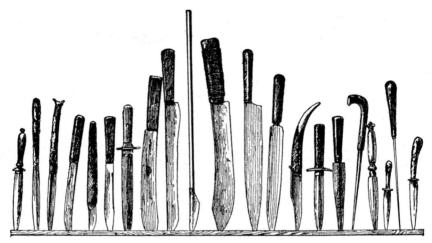

STILETTOES AND KNIVES TAKEN FROM CRIMINALS.
(From the Museum of Crime.)

A variety of stilettoes and knives confiscated from New York criminals. *Authors' collection.*

the stand, including Herbert Clark, butcher; Charles T. Carnahan, baker; George. J. Buer, baker; and David C. Myers, postmaster, all of Dennison; Michael T. Rosen and Dr. G. Conti, of Pittsburg; Henry F. Hopkins, grocer, of Cincinnati; Dr. Robert W. Chalfont; Earl N. Smith, bank cashier; and Mrs. Mary Cira, of Bellefontaine; Thomas McMahon, grocer; George Stouden, coal dealer; Alfred C. Stokes, contractor; Tracy D. Kepple, hotel keeper, all of Meadville, Pennsylvania.[366]

Mary (or Maria) Cira was the fourteen- or fifteen-year-old daughter (or step-daughter) of the late Salvatore Cira. When asked about her relationship to Collogero "Charles" Vicarrio (who had been a suspect in her father's murder), she identified herself as "Charlie's sweetheart." On one occasion when he was away in Dennison, Ohio, she was asked if she had received a letter from him every week or so. "Why I got a letter from him every day," she replied.[367] They had taken out a marriage license the previous July. Other Marion residents—bankers, blacksmiths, grocers—had their chance to put in a few good words regarding the character of the defendants as well. A bank teller, Teloa Anbauker, and Dr. Conti, both of Pittsburgh, attested to Puppino Galbo's high reputation.

Salvatore Demma (aka "Sam" DeMar) took the stand to speak on his own behalf. He said he made frequent visits to Columbus because he had a girlfriend there. While he had been in Marion on March 9, 1909, when the Black Hand conference took place, he insisted it was because he had been invited "to settle a disputed account between himself and Vincenzo Arrigo."[368] A trip to Pittsburgh the same month was even more innocent—to see an Italian doctor.

On Wednesday, spectators arriving for the trial found armed guards stationed at the top of the two stairways leading to the second-floor courtroom. For some reason, law enforcement suddenly feared an attempt would be made to rescue the defendants, so the guards were under orders not to admit any Italians or Sicilians. Joe Rinehart, the elevator man, was also cautioned about whom he allowed to enter his car.

Among the witnesses that day were bank cashier C.D. Schaffner. He examined the letters received by Amicon and stated that in his opinion they were not written by Sam Lima. However, on cross-examination, he admitted that certain letters of the alphabet were similar to those made by the accused. Similarly, Roy Zachman, another cashier, exonerated Ignoffo from the authorship of the Amicon letters. However, the testimony of Earl Sykes, a bank clerk, was disregarded because "he did not qualify as a handwriting witness."[369]

Two city detectives from Cincinnati, David Calvin "Cal" Crim and C.C. Kufer, testified about the apprehension of Francesco Spadero and Vincenzo Arrizo and certain papers found in their homes.[370] Deputy U.S. Marshal Amos F. Owens provided his account of the arrest of Ignoffo, while James D. Guest, an employee at the Athens post office, shared his knowledge of the arrests of the Limas in Marion.

Peppino Galbo claimed that the unfinished letter discovered at his house in Meadville, Pennsylvania, had been sent to him by an unknown Black Hander in New York a number of months earlier. He said he tucked it away inside his desk because he was fearful that he would be murdered if he notified the police. When he used the phrase "steaming the bananas" in a letter to Lima, he claimed he was referring to a steamship carrying a cargo of bananas.

In the months leading up to the trial, postal authorities had dropped several tantalizing claims. But once the trial began, they did not mention them again. For instance, despite J. Frank Oldfield's belief that the Arrigo-Spadera gang was connected to Giuseppe Esposito, it apparently had no bearing on the case at hand. Likewise, the possible link between Society of the Banana and the assassination of Lieutenant Petrosino was not brought up, either.[371] Again, it did not involve the U.S. mails.

The highlight of the morning session on Thursday was the introduction into evidence by District Attorney Day of a book found in Sam Lima's safe containing "The Laws and Regulations of the Society of the Banana."[372] Mary (or Maria) Lima testified that the trunk from which the book was taken belonged to a former boarder, Francesco Lima. Dated November 3, 1908, the book listed twenty-five individuals, including all fourteen defendants. Salvatore, Sebastiano and Antonio Lima, along with Giuseppe Ignoffo, were enclosed in brackets and identified as "the directorate," apparently confirming their leadership roles in the organization. The prosecution introduced testimony identifying the handwriting as Ignoffo's.

Orazio Runfola denied all the charges and attempted to explain away the suspicious passages in the letters that he and Salvatore Lima exchanged. While he acknowledged joining the Pittsburgh branch of the Society of the Banana because he hoped his friends back in Italy would think he was a big shot, he denied being the organization's president. Asked to explain the meaning of the phrase "When the machine is adjusted," he said it was an expression that meant simply "When times are better." Similarly, he claimed that when Lima commended him for "doing good work and making satisfactory collections," he was referencing his collection of money for a religious society. Many of the letters contained ambiguous references to "objects," "packages," "shipments," "medicine"—undoubtedly code words.[373] A "banana" was a letter, and "sending a banana" meant that the target had been sent a threatening letter.

The preliminary argument for the defense was made by J.P. Dawley, followed by John J. Sullivan and E.F. Guthery. District Attorney Thomas H. Gary then opened for the prosecution. Inspectors Oldfield and Pate were called for rebuttals. Assistant D.A. John H. Pratt made the final argument for the prosecution.

On Friday, the trial was delayed half an hour because one of the marshals escorting the defendants left the handcuff key in his other pair of pants. Only after the handcuffs were removed could the closing arguments begin. Attorney John O'Leary opened in the morning, arguing on behalf of his clients. He was followed by Duncan Dow, then James A. Allen. After lunch, A.F. Connolly spoke, and William A. Day summed up for the prosecution. The jury received the case at six o'clock Friday evening.

Expecting a demonstration in case of conviction, the force of deputy marshals guarding the courtroom was beefed up. They did not permit it to become overcrowded. At 10:30 Saturday morning, January 29, 1910, the jury delivered its verdict—guilty. District Attorney Day had immediately moved for sentencing.

The Amicon brothers' principal warehouse was in Columbus, Ohio. *Authors' collection.*

In handing Sam Lima sixteen years in prison, Judge Tayler said, "You seem to have been the moving spirit in this nefarious business."[374] His brother, Sebastiano Lima, and his brother-in-law, Giuseppe Ignoffo, received ten years each. All three men were residents of Marion, and many in the community were stunned. "They...claimed that the Limas worked from 18 to 20 hours every day, to make their fruit business successful, and that even then they scarcely made a good living."[375] Had they been raking in as much money as was claimed, there would have been no reason for them to work "like galley slaves, day and night."[376]

Savario Ventola of Columbus, Salvatore Demma of Bellefontaine, Antonio Vicarrio of Dennison, Collogero Vicarrio of Bellefontaine and Francesco Spadera of Cincinnati all received two-year sentences. Orazio Runfola of Pittsburgh, Pennsylvania, received six years. Peppino Galbo of Meadville, Pennsylvania, and Salvatore Arrigo of Cincinnati received four years each.

Although they had been found guilty as well, fruit dealers Augustinio Marfisi of Dennison and Vincenzo Arrigo of Cincinnati, as well as Salvatore Rizzo, a section hand from Marion, were granted new trials. In Judge Tayler's opinion, the evidence against them was weak. The court felt that "the proportion of their guilt and other circumstances would influence the length of their respective penalties."[377] While three others had also been indicted—Antonio Lima (father of Sam and Sebastiano), Sebastian Nuzzo and Giuseppe Nuzzo of Cleveland—they had escaped justice by fleeing to Italy.

The defendants accepted their sentences calmly, as did the crowd. That same afternoon, ten convicted members of the Society of the Banana and Faithful Friends were rushed to Leavenworth, Kansas, to serve their sentences. However, due to his age, twenty-year-old Antonio Vicarrio was transported to the reformatory at Elmira, New York.

Owing to the volume of threatening letters received by the post office inspectors, postmasters and district attorneys during the course of the trial, Oldfield and District Attorney Day were concerned that the prisoners' many friends might make it difficult to transport them to Leavenworth. Consequently, U.S. Marshal H.D. Davis made arrangements with the Lake Shore Company to take the prisoners to Kansas in their own private car. First, they were placed on a bus that was expected to carry them from the courtroom to the county jail. However, after a few blocks, it was diverted to the railroad car, which was parked just above Toledo's Union Station. When the train left for Kansas that afternoon, it paused to pick up the private car.

In addition to Marshal Davis, the railroad car contained eight deputies to guard against a possible assault and prevent any escape attempt. It had also been stocked with enough provisions to last until the end of the journey, courtesy of William Patterson of the Patterson Café. Patterson assigned his restaurant manager, George Randall, to oversee the operation. Randall was sworn in as a deputy as well and did double duty in looking after the meals as well as the prisoners.

On February 13, 1910, the *New York Times* proclaimed that Oldfield and the U.S. Post Office Inspection Service had proven the existence of a Black Hand organization in Ohio—the first prosecution of an organized group of criminals in United States history.

19

# THE OTHER HAND

*Mr. President: Send $5,000 or it will be the worst for you.*[378]
*—Giuseppe Pomaro*

A s far away as New Zealand, the conviction of eleven members of the Society of the Banana was news. In the *Manawatu Standard*, it was trumpeted as "the first successful prosecution of the Black Hand"—and the first successful prosecution of organized crime in America.[379] However, in St. Paul, Minnesota, the editor of the *Appeal*, an African American newspaper, saw it differently:

> *The authorities of various cities admit that they are unable to exterminate these murderous organizations and it is admitted that there is a very rapid increase in the number of undesirables, who are dumping themselves upon our shores. These murderous wretches are given rights which are denied to honest, God-fearing Afro-American citizens.*[380]

While the editor's outrage was understandable, it did not help his cause to attack another ethnic group.

Despite the (apparent) breakup of the Society of the Banana, Black Hand crime did not subside in Ohio or in the other states that purportedly constituted its territory. At trial's end, Inspector Oldfield boasted, "There has not been a sign of Black Hand operation in this section of the country since these men were arrested," conveniently overlooking the innumerable

Gene Kelly, as Johnny Columbo, sets out to avenge his father's murder in the 1950 film *Black Hand. Authors' collection.*

letters that had continued to flood the country.[381] In reality, postal inspectors would prosecute hundreds of others for Black Hand–style offenses over the next decade.

Six weeks after the trial wrapped up, the Reverend J. Adolph Cascianelli, DD, resigned the pastorate of St. Anthony's Roman Catholic Church in Canton, Ohio. He had been appointed by Monsignor Falconio, Apostolic delegate to the United States at Washington, "to investigate the Italian situation in the United States in an effort to get at the root of Italian crime, particularly black hand outrages."[382] Born in Rome, the son of a well-to-do lawyer, Cascianelli earned a PhD from the University of Rome in 1904. He was particularly devoted to the study of history and literature. Since entering the priesthood, he had been seeking an opportunity to perform missionary work.

Cascianelli anticipated that the project would require at least four years. He would be operating out of a temporary headquarters in Cleveland and slowly work his way through one diocese after another until he had covered the entire United States. Cascianelli's goal was "to increase religious restraint upon the Italians of this country in order to help them control their fiery tempers."[383] When finished, he would present the findings to Pope Pius X. The results of his personal crusade, however, were never disclosed.

Even as the Society of the Banana was being dismantled, Chicago was being wracked by Black Hand problems of its own. Two days after clothing merchant Benedetto Cinene was murdered on January 8, 1910, and one day after 194 Italians were arrested on suspicion of involvement in the crime, Joseph Noto, a friend and neighbor of the murdered man, received a Black Hand letter demanding $500 under penalty of death. When asked whether he had notified the police, Noto said he hadn't out of fear of being killed. "They don't write letters like this in Italy because they are afraid of the law."[384]

Between the first of January and the end of March, thirty-eight people were purportedly killed by Black Hand assassins in Chicago's Little Italy, many by an individual known only as Shotgun Man. The intersection of Oak and Milton Streets, where many of the killings took place, was dubbed Death's Corner. Yet despite numerous arrests, convictions continued to elude the police. But maybe law enforcement in the traditional sense wasn't the answer.

At three o'clock on the morning of June 5, 1910, Filippo (or Philippo) Catalano was leaving the Vesuvius Restaurant in Little Italy, accompanied by Edgar K. Accetta and Eugeno Monaco. As they approached a car, Monaco allegedly drew a revolver and plugged Catalano five times. A former saloonkeeper, Catalano had shot John Jocko several months earlier. However, Jocko had refused to press charges. Newspapers reported, "He was both hated and feared by his countrymen and it is believed his murder was the result of a plot."[385] Accetta, a New York lawyer, claimed he had never seen the killer before.

Catalano was murdered during the period when "Big Jim" Colosimo had summoned his nephew, Johnny "The Fox" Torrio, to rid Chicago of the Black Handers who were tormenting him. Torrio, who had been a member of New York's brutal Five Points Gang, was good at his job. In a month's time, ten Black Handers were eliminated, something neither the White Hand Society nor the Chicago Police Department had been able to do, constrained as they were by the law.

However, Giacomo "Sunny Jim" Cosmano, a rival racketeer, wasn't deterred. He demanded that Colosimo pay him $50,000 a week or he would beat up the prostitutes and customers of his brothels. Tensions between the two gangsters continued to escalate until January 18, 1912, when someone—likely Torrio—ambushed Cosmano near the Twenty-Second Street police station. Severely wounded by a shotgun blast to the stomach, Cosmano was smuggled out of the hospital and left the Windy City behind.

Black Hand operations in Columbus didn't stop, either. One of the most incredible incidents came to light on October 22, 1910, when Inspector Oldfield and a contingent of Secret Service agents and police arrested six Hungarians (not Italians) in a Columbus boardinghouse. They were charged with attempting to blackmail Archbishop Julius Van Baroosky of Kaloosa, Hungary. The archbishop had complained to Bishop Joseph J. Hartley, who asked Oldfield for help.[386] A year earlier, one Jonas Vargo had sent four letters to Baroosky, demanding payment of $12,000, to be sent to Columbus. If the archbishop did not, he would be killed and his cathedral and parochial schools destroyed. Emperor Francis Joseph of Austro-Hungary, having taken an interest in the affair, tried to apply diplomatic pressure.

The killing of Gaetano Sigano by Peter Albanese, cousin of Sergeant Peter Albanese of the Columbus police force, just before Christmas 1911, further fueled Black Hand fears. Albanese claimed Sigano had threatened to kill him and kidnap his wife on several occasions unless he paid him $50. The dead man purportedly said he wasn't collecting the money for himself but for a "mysterious brotherhood."[387] When Albanese met with the man, "he again demanded $50. I refused, and he attacked me with a butcher knife. I drew my revolver and fired twice. At the second shot, he crumbled up."[388] Immediately afterward, Albanese tried to escape but was soon overtaken. Sigano, age thirty-five, worked at the Hocking Valley Railroad roundhouse in Columbus. Albanese, in his thirties, with a wife and five children, was a foreman in the Panhandle freight yards.[389]

Seemingly no one was beyond the reach of the Black Hand. Opera singer Enrico Caruso was one of best known people in the world when he received a letter demanding $2,000. He had achieved his fame at a fortuitous time: the phonograph industry was just getting started and people all over the world were able to hear the fabled tenor sing for mere pennies—pennies which translated into more than $2 million in earnings. But the money meant little to Caruso (he sometimes earned as much as $7,000 a performance), who paid the blackmailers in the hope that they would leave him alone. However, the attendant publicity inspired other blackmailers. Then, early in March, Caruso received two more letters ordering him to place $15,000 under the stoop of a factory in Sacket Street, Brooklyn. Although generous by nature, Caruso was not a fool. This time he went directly to the police.

Opera singer Enrico Caruso was one of the most famous people targeted by the Black Hand. *Library of Congress.*

On March 4, 1910, "A trap was laid."[390] Caruso explained how he was directed to prepare a decoy envelope with a dollar bill wrapped around a wad of paper. He then gave it to his valet to place at the prearranged location at about 10:40 p.m. Lieutenant Gloster of the Italian bureau and two of his lieutenants had been hiding inside the factory since nine o'clock while two other men concealed themselves in the shadows.

When Misiani and another man were reaching for the package, Antonio Cincotta quickly approached and told them to flee. Cincotta then ran into a saloon operated by the notorious Lupo gang, where Gloster and his men captured him. Meanwhile, Misiani was caught by Officers Simonette and Scrivani just as he dropped a sawed-off shotgun and was struggling to pull a revolver out of his pocket. While awaiting trial, Misiani jumped bail and was not recaptured.

Given Caruso's celebrity, the trial couldn't help but be a sensation. Asked by Misiani's attorney what he did for a living, he replied, "Oh, I sing a little, at times."[391] He admitted he was "Not exactly tickled" when the blackmailers demanded the money.[392] It was a great show for everyone except the defendant, even though he had one of the best seats. Sentenced to prison, Cincotta was released in December 1914.

Then early on February 16, 1915, two men stepped out of a Brooklyn doorway, shot Cincotta three times in the stomach and left him to die. It was just one block from where Cincotta and three others had killed a man named Serro in May 1896 because he had testified against a compatriot. Although Cincotta had many enemies, it was widely believed he was killed for trying to shake down Caruso. Nevertheless, Caruso continued to receive Black Hand threats the rest of his life.

Even the president of the United States was not immune. A Youngstown steel worker, Giuseppe Pomaro, was arrested on June 7, 1913, by Captain John E. Washer of the U.S. Secret Service. He was charged with having written President Woodrow Wilson a Black Hand letter demanding $5,000. It read:

> *Mr. Wilson, President of the U.S., Washington, D.C.*
> *Mr. President: Send $5,000 or it will be the worst for you.*
> *Giuseppe Pomaro*
> *28 North Watt St.*[393]

Although he had signed his name, thirty-five-year-old Pomaro, an Italian immigrant, denied any guilt. The letter contained no specific threat, but it did have a Black Hand doodle beneath the signature. It instructed Wilson to deposit the money in Pomaro's name in a local Italian bank. "According to Washer, Pomaro had visited the bank several times during the last week acting as though he expected some communication."[394]

Later, Pomaro confessed, "saying he 'just wanted money.'"[395] Various newspapers reported "that Pomaro is one of a black hand band operating in this section and having connections in New York as the eastern end, and reaching through this district from Pittsburgh, Newcastle, East Youngstown and Cleveland."[396] A recent demand of $2,000 from Anthony Parilla, a well-to-do Italian in Youngstown, was thought to have been the work of the same gang.

This was not the end of Wilson's Black Hand woes, however. A couple of years later, Captain Washer charged James Spana (or Scano) of Youngstown, Ohio, with being the author of a letter sent to President Wilson, again demanding money.[397] Spana was placed in the Cuyahoga County jail on January 6, 1915. He was arrested the day before when he called at the Youngstown post office to inquire for a letter from his mother in Cavalona, Italy. Spana had previously been implicated in the sending of other Black Hand letters. Two years before, he lost the use of his left hand from a knife wound in the arm sustained during a fight, but he could still write threatening letters with the other.

In September 1911, thirteen months after entering the U.S. Penitentiary at Leavenworth, Kansas, Salvatore Demma, Collogero Vicarrio, Savario Ventola and Francesco Spadera—four convicted members of the Society of the Banana and Faithful Friends—were paroled. At the time of their release, the men ranged in age from twenty-seven to forty-eight. They promptly departed for Cleveland before dispersing. Ventola is known to have returned to Columbus and Galbo to Meadville. When he reached Bellefontaine, Vicarrio went directly to the home of his fiancée, Maria "Mary" Cira, and then to the courthouse to obtain a marriage license. After that, nothing further was heard of any of them. Whether they changed their names, returned to Italy or turned over a new leaf is unknown.

About a year later, on August 8, 1912, "Six detectives and two patrolmen surrounded a brick house at 614 Carlisle Avenue [in Cincinnati]…and arrested nine Italians as alleged Black Hand men."[398] The arrests resulted from the stabbing of an Italian behind a house on Plum Street. A thorough search of the dwelling turned up "ammunition of all kinds; ice picks converted into weapons, blackjacks, and twined nooses, which the police say are like those used by the Paris Apaches."[399] Secreted in the clothing of the

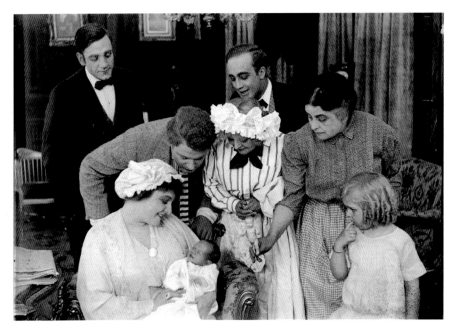

Seven-year-old Runa Hodges starred in the 1915 movie *Runa and the Black Hand*. *Billy Rose Theatre Collection, New York Public Library.*

suspects were various weapons, including revolvers and stilettos fashioned from long files.

Having taken the conspirators by surprise, the officers confiscated various books, papers and correspondence as evidence. Among the letters was one addressed to a fellow gang member, putting him on notice that he could expect to soon feel a bullet in his stomach for informing the police. All of the men taken into custody during the Cincinnati raid were said to belong to the Society of the Banana. What, if any, connection this band had with the earlier group of that name is unknown. Regardless, there was no further mention of the once notorious outfit.

Marion threatened to become another Black Hand stronghold in 1915, but by the 1920s, all such activities had been supplanted by the rise of the American gangster and large-scale organized crime in response to Prohibition. While people still received threatening letters warning them to pay up or else, the specter of a Black Hand Society was no longer taken seriously by the public, the press or law enforcement.

Meanwhile, the produce company founded by John Amicon had fallen on hard times. In February 1928, the company entered "friendly receivership" so that his elder brother, Charles, who had been suffering from ill health, could withdraw from the business.[400] John would remain as head of the firm, continuing to receive and distribute bulk lots of fruits and vegetables for seven more years. He would pass away in 1937 at the age of sixty-eight, two years after the company went bankrupt. Charles followed him in death a year later at age seventy-three.

By then, the Black Hand had been relegated to a footnote in history, but Hollywood wasn't quite done with it yet. In the 1950 crime drama *Black Hand*, song-and-dance man Gene Kelly took on the Black Hand Society in a non-musical turn. Set in New York's "Little Italy," it concerned an Italian named Giovanni "Johnny" Columbo who had sworn a vendetta against the group for the murder of his father, but after falling for a childhood friend, Isabella Gomboli (Teresa Celli), and meeting an honest cop, Louis Lorelli, he began to consider seeking his revenge through the justice system. Although fictional, the film did incorporate some episodes from the life of Lieutenant Petrosino, on whom Lorelli (played by J. Carrol Naish) was based. The film was released just in time to take advantage of the publicity generated by the Kefauver Committee.

In 1950–51, the Senate Special Committee to Investigate Crime in Interstate Commerce examined organized crime activity following World War II. Headed by Senator Estes Kefauver, the committee reviewed (among many other things) various newspaper clippings, documents and other exhibits provided by the chief post office inspector pertaining specifically to the Society of the Banana and the events of 1909.

In the General Conclusions of the *Third Interim Report*, May 1, 1951, the committee declared:

> *There is a sinister criminal organization known as the Mafia operating throughout the country with ties in other nations, in the opinion of the committee. The Mafia is the direct descendant of a criminal organization of the same name originating in the island of Sicily. In this country, the Mafia has also been known as the Black Hand and the Unione Siciliano* [sic].

Throughout the Kefauver Committee's inquiry, J. Edgar Hoover, director of the Federal Bureau of Investigation, refused to cooperate. Not only did he deny the existence of an Italian American Mafia, but he refused to believe that any sort of criminal syndicate or organization played a significant role in American crime as well.[401] It was "merely a loose collection of independent racketeers."[402] Consequently, he did not devote the FBI's resources to probing such matters until ordered to do so by Attorney General Robert Kennedy in 1961. And somehow what had once been an accepted fact—that the Society of the Banana and Faithful Friends was the first organized crime enterprise successfully prosecuted in the United States—was lost to history.

# BYLAWS AND REGULATIONS

*Were it not for the atrocious character of the rules and the prescribed penalties for their violation this might seem almost a joke.
But the "Society of the Banana and Faithful Friends" appears from the constitution to be no eleemosynary institution.*[403]
—Washington (D.C.) Evening Star

Sergeant Victor P. Churches of the Columbus Police Department was often called on to translate the letters and other documents captured in the Marion raid. Presumably, it was his translation of "Bylaws and Regulations of the Society of the Banana" that appeared in the *Marion Daily Mirror* and elsewhere.[404]

Art. 1 The person who tries to reveal the secrets of this society will be punished with death.

Art. 2. A member who offends one of his companions, staining his honor, will be punished according to Article 1.

Art. 3. The member who tries to do harm to another branch of the society or to the family of other companions, if this harm shall have been grave, will be undressed and marked on his body with the marks of infamy, and called with words of contempt "Swindler," and if the offense is more grave he will be stabbed.

Art. 4. The person who is a coward and does not sustained the punishment assigned to him by the society, will be punished in accordance with Article 3.

Art. 5. The member who profits by the opportunity of a plan of another member, is punished as prescribed in Art. 3. If the misdemeanor is less grave he must make restitution within 24 hours of that which he caused to be lost, and he will be cut off from his share of the profits for two months.

Art. 6. The member who offends another companion with offensive titles, if the offense is considered grave, will not only lose his right of membership, but will also be stabbed. If the offense is less grave, he will be cut off from his share of the profits for three months and at the same time must do his duty.

Art. 7. The member who has received the insult and resents it himself without notifying the society, is punished accordingly to Art. 3.

Art 8. The member who abandons one of his companions in the time of need will be held to be a traitor and then punished according to Art. 3.

Art. 9. The person appointed to inspect must always go around and maintain good order as it is prescribed, passing all the news around. Failing in this for the first time, he will be cut off from his share of the profits for three months, the second time he will he stabbed.

Art. 10. A reunion of the society cannot be called for a visiting member if he is not known.

Art. 11. The person who goes away must pass the news and tell the "local" in the place where he goes, how long he will be there, and if he carries a message he must leave his pledge. Failing to do this he will be punished according to Art. 6.

Art. 12. The person who shall have been called to use the knife and does not, through fear, will be punished according to Art. 3.

Art. 13. The person who deals sparingly (does not do his duty) will be punished according to Art. 3 at a convenient place by the society with a brand in his face.

Art. 14. The person who refutes the call of command will, for the first time, be deprived of his share for three months; for the second time from one to three cuts with the knife; for the third time, from two to five cuts, as the society thinks best, and to follow his work as prescribed; if it be grave he will be punished according to Art. 3, without having any benefits from the society.

Art. 15. The person who is sent somewhere by the society will be paid by the day and for the journey.

Art. 16. There can be no excuse for failures or penalties in conformity with the articles. However, there may be extenuating circumstances in case of drunkenness.

# NOTES

## Introduction

1. "More Evidence Is Secured Against Suspected Black Hand," *Marion (OH) Daily Mirror,* June 9, 1909.
2. For example, the *Boston Weekly News-Letter* reported in the March 20–28, 1740, issue that eight or ten Irishmen had invaded the home of a man of some means and murdered him, his daughter and his servants. His wife escaped detection by hiding in a hogshead of feathers.
3. Cawthorne, *Mafia.*
4. D'Amato, "'Black Hand' Myth."
5. Ibid.
6. Schiavo, *Truth About the Mafia.*
7. Technically true, but only because the Mafiosi never refer to themselves as "the Mafia."
8. Sherman Alexie calls himself an Indian (not a Native American), and that's good enough for me.

## Chapter 1

9. Evans, "Crimes of Mafia."
10. Persico, "Vendetta in New Orleans."
11. Ibid.

NOTES TO PAGES 17–28

12. "Chief Hennessy Avenged," *New York Times*, March 15, 1891.
13. Nelli, *Business of Crime.*
14. Baiamonte,"'Who Killa de Chief' Revisited."
15. Hendley, *American Gangsters.*
16. Devereaux had a grudge against Mike Hennessy, which led to a shootout, during which David Hennessy shot him in the back of the head.
17. Baiamonte, "'Who Killa de Chief' Revisited."
18. Ibid.
19. Although Italy had been unified into one country, many of its citizens still maintained their regional identities.
20. The Pinkerton Detective Agency was founded by William's father, Allan Pinkerton.
21. "More Threats by the Mafia," *Indianapolis (IN) Journal*, March 18, 1891.
22. Morgan, "What Shall We Do with the Dago?."
23. Baiamonte, "'Who Killa de Chief' Revisited."
24. Persico, "Vendetta in New Orleans."
25. Gambino, *Vendetta.*
26. Persico, "Vendetta in New Orleans."
27. Woodwiss, *Organized Crime and American Power.*
28. Gaster initiated the practice of wearing his badge upside down to set himself apart from the other members of the police force.

## Chapter 2

29. Falco, "When Italian Immigrants Were 'The Other.'"
30. Gambino, *Vendetta.*
31. Nelli, *Business of Crime.*
32. "In Italy," *Logan (UT) Republican*, February 24, 1906.
33. Italians still tended to identify themselves by geographical regions.
34. Parrington, *Beginnings of Critical Realism.*
35. "Coming Over the Water," *Daily Evening Bulletin (Maysville, KY)*, August 23, 1887.
36. *Ward County (ND) County Independent*, January 24, 1907.
37. On the other hand, Franklin was quite fond of the French.
38. Franklin, *Observation Concerning the Increase.*
39. *Greensboro (NC) Times*, October 27, 1860.
40. Smith and Edmonston, eds., *New Americans.*
41. Ibid.

42. Wilson, *History of the American People*.
43. Ibid.
44. White, "Passing of the Black Hand Society."
45. Oppenheimer, "Nationality of New York Criminals."
46. Ibid.

## Chapter 3

47. "The Mafia," *Columbus (OH) Dispatch*, February 5, 1895.
48. Ibid.
49. Ibid.
50. Ibid.
51. Durante felt that the Democratic Party's support of slavery represented a betrayal of the working man.
52. "The Mafia," *Columbus (OH) Dispatch*.
53. He is best remembered for the famous Johnny Marzetti casserole popularized in school cafeterias.
54. The Columbus Italian Unit may have predated that of New York City and the Pinkertons.
55. "The Mafia," *Columbus (OH) Dispatch*.
56. "An Ohio Mafia," *Daily Public Ledger (Maysville, KY)*, February 6, 1895.
57. "The Mafia," *Columbus (OH) Dispatch*.
58. "After the Dagos," *Columbus (OH) Evening Dispatch*, May 7, 1889.
59. "Mafia's Code in New-York," *New York Times*, May 16, 1893.
60. Newton, *Mafia at Apalachin*.
61. "'Barrel' Murder Plot and Victim Known," *New York Times*, April 21, 1903.
62. Willis, *Wise Guys*.
63. "'Black Hand' Band in Extortion Plot," *New York Herald*, September 13, 1903.
64. Ibid.
65. "'Black Hand' Is Threatening Again," *(New York) Evening World*, September 17, 1903.
66. Ibid.
67. "Live in Constant Fear," *New York Times*, September 14, 1903.
68. "Italian Girl Stabs Husband and Wife," *New York Times*, February 24, 1906.
69. Nelli, *Business of Crime*.

70. "'Black Hand' Extortionists," *New York Times*, December 4, 1903.
71. Ibid.
72. "Important Witness Disappears," *Indianapolis (IN) Journal*, December 8, 1903.
73. "Informer Is Victim of Mafia," *San Francisco (CA) Call*, December 14, 1903.

## Chapter 4

74. "New York Children," *Barbour County (KS) Index*, September 7, 1904.
75. "The 'Black Hand' Again," *New York Times*, January 18, 1904.
76. "'Black Hand' Death Threat," *New York Times*, February 29, 1904.
77. "Letter from 'Black Hand'," *New York Times*, March 8, 1904.
78. "Ciro Declared Victim of Blackmailer's Plot," *New York Times*, July 29, 1904.
79. Ibid.
80. Ibid.
81. "Bomb Hurled into a Crime," *New York Times*, August 8, 1904.
82. "Black Hand Society," *Ohio Democrat*, August 11, 1904.
83. "Police Link Kidnapping with Barrel Murder," *New York Times*, August 13, 1904.
84. Pittsburgh was generally spelled "Pittsburg" in those days.
85. Ibid.
86. "May Have Been Mannino Boy," *New York Times*, August 16, 1904.
87. "Black Hand," *Stark County (OH) Democrat*, August 23, 1904.
88. *Perrysburg (OH) Journal*, August 19, 1904.
89. Ibid.
90. "Threat from 'Black Hand'," *New York Times*, August 14, 1904.
91. Ibid.
92. So named by Police Captain Alexander "Clubber" Williams.
93. "Would Shoot 'Black Hand'," *New York Times*, August 16, 1904.
94. Ibid.
95. "Black Hand Foiled," *New York Times*, August 17, 1904.
96. "New Black Hand Letter," *New York Times*, August 17, 1904.

## Chapter 5

97. White, "Passing of the Black Hand Society."

98. Newton, *Mafia at Apalachin*.

99. "Police Now Fear Hand of Vendetta," *Columbus (OH) Press-Post*, April 27, 1904.

100. "Shot from Above," *Columbus (OH) Citizen*, April 28, 1904.

101. They Feared Maffia," *(Columbus, OH) Press Post*, January 6, 1905.

102. "Vendetta Pursues Falconi to Italy," *Columbus (OH) Citizen*, January 6, 1905.

103. "Bloody Deed of Italian Mafia," *Fort Wayne (IN) News*, April 27, 1904.

104. Ibid.

105. Ibid.

106. "Wrong Name," *(Columbus, OH) Press Post*, October 18, 1905. Note "Nollied" means to dismiss.

107. "Murderer Captured," *Columbus (OH) Press-Post*, July 28, 1907.

108. "Resenting an Insult," *Perrysburg (OH) Journal*, October 14, 1904.

109. "Mafia in Existence," *(Columbus, OH) Press Post*, October 20, 1904.

110. Although he was frequently called upon for his "expertise," Coroner Joseph "Suicide" Murphy was not an especially astute investigator.

111. "Murders by the Mafia," *Bristol (IN) Banner*, October 28, 1904.

## Chapter 6

112. Whiteside, *Italy in the Nineteenth Century*.

113. "The Mafia," *Stark County (OH) Democrat*, January 13, 1905.

114. "Shot During Family Row," *Columbus (OH) Citizen*, January 23, 1905.

115. "Italian Marked by 'Black' Hand Society," *Columbus (OH) Press-Post*, March 21, 1905.

116. "Italians Renew Old Feud," *Columbus (OH) Press-Post*, June 1, 1906.

117. "Black Hand Breaks Out," *Columbus (OH) Press-Post*, July 24, 1905.

118. "Rich Italian Quails Before 'Black Hand'," *Washington (D.C.) Times*, August 27, 1905.

119. "Blackmailers Hurl Bomb at Victim's Home," *(New York) Evening World*, August 31, 1905.

120. "Camp in Ice Box Thirteen Hours," *San Francisco (CA) Call*, February 17, 1906.

121. "Investigate the 'Mafia'," *Columbus (OH) Press-Post*, November 8, 1906

## Chapter 7

122. *Columbus (OH) Press-Post*, April 13, 1908.

123. The urgency was due to the cost of guarding the suspect and the Grasso brothers, as well as Sheriff E.E. Drown's fear that an attempt would be made to dynamite the county jail.

124. "Guiffrita Is Shot to Death," *Marion (OH) Star*, November 24, 1906.

125. "Gioffritta Murder Trial," *Marion (OH) Daily Mirror*, January 30, 1907.

126. When Cornwell abruptly resigned three years later, he was roundly praised for having elevated the professionalism of the Marion Police Department.

127. "Funeral of Late Louis Guiffritta," *Marion (OH) Star*, November 27, 1906.

128. Ibid.

129. Ibid.

130. Ibid.

131. DeMar's headstone at Calvary Cemetery in Bellefontaine lists his name as "Antonino Demma," and he may have been Syrian, rather than Italian.

132. "Vendetta Claims a Boy as Victim," *Cairo (IL) Bulletin*, March 27, 1907.

133. "Black Hand Murder in Ohio," *Warren (OH) Sheaf*, March 28, 1907.

134. "Vendetta Claims a Boy as Victim," *Cairo (IL) Bulletin*.

135. Ibid.

136. "Italian Merchant and the Tragedy," *Greenville (OH) Journal*, April 16, 1908.

137. *Columbus (OH) Press-Post*, April 13, 1908.

138. Ibid.

139. Ibid.

140. Ibid.

141. "He Prayed 'for Strength'," *Marion (OH) Daily Mirror*, April 13, 1908.

142. *Columbus (OH) Press-Post*, April 13, 1908.

143. Possibly he was confused with Charlie DeMar.

## Chapter 8

144. *Marion (OH) Daily Mirror*, July 26, 1907.

145. "Witness Given 'Signal of Death'," *Bismarck (ND) Daily Tribune*, June 19, 1907.

146. Ibid.

147. "Black Hand Trailed," *(Washington, D.C.) Evening Star*, August 7, 1909.

148. Ibid.
149. Cawthorne, *Mafia.*
150. Lombardo, *Black Hand.*
151. Willis, *Wise Guys.*
152. Woods, "In the Grip."
153. Nelli, *Business of Crime.*
154. Ibid.
155. Hale, "Menace of the Black Hand."
156. Ibid.
157. "Baltimore Black Hand," *New York Tribune,* January 19, 1908.
158. "Black Hand in Cleveland," *Urbana (IL) Daily Courier,* January 9, 1908.
159. Chief Pumphrey would later be forced to resign due to unscrupulous behavior in office.
160. Hale, "Menace of the Black Hand."
161. "Baltimore Black Hand," *New York Tribune.*
162. "School for Assassins," *(Washington, D.C.) Evening Star,* December 25, 1907.
163. Ibid.
164. "Black Hand at Bellaire," *Fairmont West Virginian,* July 9, 1907.
165. "Government Is Being Blamed," *Cairo (IL) Bulletin,* December 27, 1907.

## *Chapter 9*

166. "Review of the World," *Current Literature* 46, no. 5 (May 1909).
167. Ibid.
168. Oppenheimer, "Nationality of New York Criminals."
169. "Black Hand in Cleveland," *Urbana (IL) Daily Courier.*
170. "The Fake Black Hand in Chicago," *Manchester (IA) Democrat,* June 16, 1909.
171. "A Dynamite Scare," *Mahoning (OH) Dispatch,* November 20, 1908.
172. "Freed on Technicality," *Ohio State Journal,* February 9, 1909.
173. "Review of the World."
174. The surname is also spelled Coluccio, Cossucio, Colluchi and Callouchi, but we have settled on Colluccio.
175. *Columbus (OH) Dispatch,* June 14, 1907.
176. Ibid.
177. This was the heart of the city's "The Badlands," a notorious neighborhood.
178. *Columbus (OH) Press-Post,* February 4, 1908.

179. *Columbus (OH) Press-Post*, September 14, 1908.
180. "Affidavits," *Stark County (OH) Democrat*, February 7, 1908.
181. Ibid.
182. "Italian Held to Grand Jury for Extortion," *Stark County (OH) Democrat*, February 11, 1908.
183. Ibid.
184. "Money or Life," *Columbus (OH) Press-Post*, May 22, 1908.
185. Ibid.
186. Ibid.
187. $30,000 would be about $750,000 in 2017.
188. "Other Victims," *Columbus (OH) Evening Dispatch*, June 9, 1909.
189. *Columbus (OH) Post Press*, April 4, 1908.
190. Ibid.
191. "Black Hand Again Busy," *Perrysburg (OH) Journal*, April 10, 1908.

## Chapter 10

192. Denison, "Black Hand."
193. Ibid.
194. Ironically, Detective Frank Dimaio is best known today for leading the posse that tracked down Butch Cassidy and the Sundance Kid in the movie of the same name.
195. "Petrosini, the Italian Detective," *Washington (D.C.) Post*, January 20, 1907.
196. Ibid.
197. "Form Society to Wipe Out Black Hand," *(Astoria, OR) Morning Astorian*, September 25, 1908.
198. Lombardo, *Black Hand*.
199. "The White Hand Society," *La Tribuna Italiana (Chicago, IL)*, February 22, 1908.
200. "White Hand Will Fight Black Hand," *Aberdeen (SD) Democrat*, January 3, 1908.
201. Lombardo, *Black Hand*.
202. Sifakis, *The Mafia Encyclopedia*.
203. "White Hand Fights with Black Hand," *New York Times*, December 10, 1907.
204. "New Wrinkle in Insurance," *Pensacola (FL) Journal*, July 22, 1908.
205. The image of bomb-throwing anarchists was cemented in the public mind when they struck Wall Street a dozen years later.

206. "White Hand Society Threatens," *Topeka (KS) Daily Capital,* January 12, 1908.

207. "Says His Death Is Sought," *Chicago (IL) Tribune,* July 6, 1909.

## Chapter 11

208. "Succeeds in Breaking Up Murderous Black Hand," *Cook County (MN) Herald,* November 16, 1907.

209. "Besieged in Their Stronghold," *(Hillsboro, OH) News-Herald,* September 6, 1906.

210. Ibid.

211. Ibid.

212. "Three Men Killed in a Fight," *(Reynoldsburg, PA) Star,* September 5, 1906.

213. Ibid.

214. "Was a Black Hand Victim," *Fairmont West Virginian,* December 27, 1906.

215. "Tables Turned on Black Hand," *(Sycamore, IL) True Republican,* April 24, 1907.

216. Implicated in one of New York's "barrel murders," Perino moved to Browntown after being released from prison.

217. "Black Hand," *Marion (OH) Daily Mirror,* April 29, 1907.

218. Ibid.

219. "Plot Within a Plot," *(Marshalltown, IA) Evening Times-Republican,* April 26, 1907.

220. "Criminal Safe if They Reached 'Helltown'," *Fairmont West Virginian,* July 29, 1907.

221. Ibid.

222. "U.S. Steel Corporation Runs Down Worst Gang of Assassins Known," *Bisbee (AZ) Daily Review,* August 1, 1907.

223. *Marion (OH) Daily Mirror,* July 26, 1907.

224. "School for Murderers," *Salina (KS) Daily Union,* August 24, 1907.

225. "U.S. Steel Corporation Runs Down," *Bisbee (AZ) Daily Review.*

226. "Black Hand Gang Is Run to Earth," *Chicago (IL) Sunday Tribune,* August 4, 1907.

227. *Perrysburg (OH) Journal,* October 18, 1907.

228. "Succeeds in Breaking Up Murderous Black Hand," *Cook County (MN) Herald.*

## Chapter 12

229. Harden, *Passage to America*.

230. "Black Hand Members on Carpet," *Montrose (CO) Daily Press*, December 6, 1909.

231. Harden, *Passage to America*.

232. "Black Hand Explosion," *Indianapolis (IN) News*, May 13, 1908.

233. As early as 1893, Amicon was advertising that Santa Claus had made his store his Christmas headquarters.

234. O'Neil, *Diocese of Columbus*.

235. A third brother, Anthony, also lived in Columbus, but apparently did not work with them.

236. The magazine is a designated storage room for explosive material.

237. "Running Down the Black Hand," *New York Times*, February 13, 1910.

238. "Catch Black Hand Men," *Ohio State Journal*, January 19, 1909.

239. "Pays $1000 to 'Black Hand'," *Ohio State Journal*, February 2, 1909.

240. "Black Hand Warning," *Ohio State Journal*, February 14, 1909.

241. "Black Handers Say They Will Eat His Heart," *Columbus (OH) Citizen*, August 7, 1909.

242. Columbus had two Italian sergeants at the time.

243. "Arrest Many Suspects for Petrosino Murder," *Columbus (OH) State Journal*, March 17, 1909.

244. Writer Arrigo Petacco claimed that while imprisoned in 1930, Cascioferro said, "In my whole life I have killed only one person, and I did that disinterestedly….Petrosino was a brave adversary, and deserved better than a shameful death at the hands of some hired cut-throat."

245. Ibid.

246. "Italian Police Proffer No Aid," *Ohio State Journal*, March 15, 1909.

## Chapter 13

247. "Black Hand Leaders," *(Washington, D.C.) Evening Star*, June 12, 1909.

248. "Black Hand Trial Is Begun," *New York Times*, January 20, 1910.

249. "Again Put Through Sweating Process," *(Wilmington, DE) Evening Journal*, May 2, 1902.

250. "More Evidence Is Secured," *Marion (OH) Daily Mirror*.

251. In 1933, "Uncle George" Pate would retire to his home in Youngstown, Ohio, after thirty-two years on the job.

252. "Watched Through Hole in Wall," *Santa Fe New Mexican,* June 10, 1909.

253. The surname is also spelled Vicario and Viccario, but we have settled on Vicarrio.

254. "Running Down the Black Hand Band," *(Washington, D.C.) Evening Star,* June 9, 1909.

255. "Suspect Fellow Passengers," *Ohio State Journal,* March 17, 1909.

256. "Black Hand Appears Inactive in Pittsburgh," *Pittsburgh (PA) Daily Post,* March 14, 1909.

257. "Black Hand Is Declared Myth," *Bismarck (ND) Daily Tribune,* April 17, 1909.

258. Ibid.

259. "Grocer Is Threatened," *Ohio State Journal,* April 18, 1909.

260. "Gets Black Hand Letter," *Ohio State Journal,* April 19, 1909.

261. "Fighting the Black Hand," *Marion (OH) Daily Mirror,* April 23, 1909.

262. "Cut Flesh from Man When Refused Money," *Ohio State Journal,* April 20, 1909.

263. "Threaten Rich Man's Life," *(Cresco, IA) Twice-A-Week Plain Dealer,* May 7, 1909.

264. "Newark Has Black Hand Sensation," *Columbus (OH) Press-Post,* May 4, 1909.

265. "Murder May Be Traced to Black Hand," *Marion (OH) Daily Mirror,* May 18, 1909.

## Chapter 14

266. "Black Hand Investigation Is Widening," *(Grand Forks, ND) Evening Times,* June 10, 1909.

267. Inspector W.L. Owens is mentioned, but his exact involvement is unknown.

268. Some accounts erroneously stated it was Joe and Sam Rizzo's store.

269. "Marion Is the Headquarters for the Black Hand Gang," *Marion (OH) Daily Mirror,* June 8, 1909.

270. "More Evidence Is Secured," *Marion (OH) Daily Mirror.*

271. Ibid.

272. "State May Try Black Handers," *Marion (OH) Daily Mirror,* June 10, 1909.

273. Wright later became a successful screenwriter in Hollywood.

274. Wright, "Conflict with the 'Black Hand'."

275. Ibid.
276. Ibid.
277. Ibid.
278. Ibid.
279. Ibid.
280. Although it was also spelled Collergio and Collergrio, we have settled on Collogero.
281. Wright, "Conflict with the 'Black Hand'."
282. Ibid.
283. Ibid.
284. "Caught at Bellefontaine," *Urbana (OH) Daily Courier*, June 10, 1909.
285. "Arrest of Charles Viccario Regarded as a Go-Between," *(Washington, D.C.) Evening Star*, June 9, 1909.
286. While the surname is also spelled Nusso or Neuzzo, we have settled on Nuzzo. And they seemed to have been Giuseppe ("Joseph") and Antonio.
287. *Columbus (OH) Post Press*, March 24, 1908.
288. Ibid.
289. "State May Try Black Handers," *Marion (OH) Daily Mirror*.
290. About $75,000 in 2017.
291. "Arrest Alleged Black Hands," *Fruit Trade Journal and Produce Record*, June 12, 1909.
292. "Blackhand Leaders Trapped in Ohio," *New York Times*, June 9, 1909.
293. Ibid.
294. "Arrest Alleged Black Hands," *Fruit Trade Journal*.
295. Often translated as "youth of honor."
296. This is the "made man" in Mafia terminology.
297. "More Evidence Is Secured," *Marion (OH) Daily Mirror*.
298. "Black Hand Band a National Order," *New York Times*, June 10, 1909.
299. "Two Well Armed Italians," *Columbus (OH) Evening Dispatch*, June 15, 1909.
300. "Postal Inspectors Make a Big Haul," *Chillicothe (OH) Gazette*, June 9, 1909.

## Chapter 15

301. *Columbus (OH) Dispatch*, June 9, 1909.
302. "More Evidence Is Secured," *Marion (OH) Daily Mirror*.
303. Lima's bond was paid by Antonio Cangiamilla, a wealthy commission merchant.
304. *New York Times*, June 11, 1909.

305. *Columbus (OH) Dispatch,* June 9, 1909.
306. "Society of the Banana," *(New York) Sun,* June 13, 1909.
307. "Another Raid Made by Federal Officers," *Marion (OH) Daily Mirror,* June 14, 1909.
308. Ibid.
309. *New York Times,* June 16, 1909.
310. "May be Traced to Doors of Foreigners," *Marion (OH) Daily Mirror,* June 16, 1909.
311. Ibid.
312. *New York Times,* June 13, 1909.
313. A couple of Cincinnati banana peddlers were arrested on September 1, 1886, and charged with giving out counterfeit money in change.
314. *New York Times,* June 19, 1909.
315. "More Black Hand Arrests," *New York Times,* June 18, 1909.
316. "Brains of the Black Hand," *(New York) Sun,* June 20, 1909.
317. Ibid.
318. "Liberty Is Death for Squealer," *Cincinnati (OII) Enquirer,* June 22, 1909.
319. "Two Arrests at Pittsburgh," *(Washington. D.C.) Evening Star,* December 12, 1909.
320. "Black Hand Clues in Petrosino Plot," *New York Times,* August 7, 1909.
321. "Runfola Hearing To-day," *Pittsburgh (PA) Daily Post,* June 21, 1909.
322. Ibid.

## Chapter 16

323. *New York Times,* September 12, 1909.
324. "Black Hands Are Still Doing Biz," *Bismarck (ND) Daily Tribune,* June 15, 1909.
325. "Black Hand Defies Federal Detectives," *Los Angeles (CA) Herald,* June 15, 1909.
326. Savario Ventola is sometimes mistakenly listed as Salvatore Ventola.
327. "Black Hand Society Guilty of Crimes," *Pensacola (FL) Journal,* June 10, 1909.
328. "Held," *Cincinnati (OH) Enquirer,* July 3, 1909.
329. "Lima Store Now Closed," *Marion (OH) Daily Mirror,* July 22, 1909.
330. Ibid.
331. "Arrigo Found in Lonely Cabin and Placed Under Arrest by Federal Officers," *Cincinnati (OH) Enquirer,* July 24, 1909.

332. Ibid.

333. "Revealed Hiding Place of Arrigo," *Cincinnati (OH) Enquirer*, July 25, 1909.

334. "Arrigo Found in Lonely Cabin," *Cincinnati (OH) Enquirer*.

335. "Revealed Hiding Place of Arrigo," *Cincinnati (OH) Enquirer*.

336. "Macaroni His Undoing," *Urbana (OH) Daily Courier*, July 28, 1909.

337. *(Hillsboro, OH) News-Herald*, July 29, 1909.

338. "Black Hand Clues in Petrosino Plot," *New York Times*, August 7, 1909.

339. "Black Hand Gang Supplicant for Victims' Mercy," *Columbus (OH) Sunday Dispatch*, August 8, 1909.

340. "Black Hand Clues in Petrosino Plot," *New York Times*.

341. "Hope to Convict," *New Ulm (MN) Review*, June 16, 1909.

342. "Black Hand Members on Carpet," *Montrose (CO) Daily Press*.

343. "Black Hand Trailed," *(Washington D.C.) Evening Star*, August 7, 1909.

344. Ibid.

345. "The Black Hand Society," *The New York Times*, August 9, 1909.

346. Ibid.

347. "Joe Ignoffo Is Arrested," *Marion (OH) Daily Mirror*, December 1, 1909.

348. Ibid.

349. "Syrian Under Arrest," *(Washington, D.C.) Evening Star*, December 5, 1909.

350. "16 Black Hand Indictments," *(New York) Sun*, December 12, 1909.

## Chapter 17

351. *Literary Digest*, 38, no. 25 (June 19, 1909).

352. Judge Tayler would die ten months later at the age of fifty-eight.

353. "See Imprint of the Black Hand in the Killing of John Resasco," *Columbus (OH) Press-Post*, January 13, 1910.

354. "Black Hand Trial Is Begun," *New York Times*.

355. "Sleuth Exposes the Black Hand Methods," *Marion (OH) Star*, January 21, 1910.

356. For three months, the Amicon brothers paid seventy-five to one hundred dollars a month each for detectives to watch out over them.

357. "Sleuth Exposes the Black Hand Methods," *Marion (OH) Star*.

358. "Tell of Paying the Money Over to Band," *Marion (OH) Star*, January 22, 1910.

## Chapter 18

359. *New York Times*, February 13, 1910.
360. "Black Handers Held Under Bond," *Marion (OH) Daily Mirror*, June 29, 1909.
361. "More Evidence Is Secured," *Marion (OH) Daily Mirror*.
362. "All Letters Are Admitted," *Marion (OH) Daily Mirror*, January 25, 1910.
363. During the Black Hand frenzy, it was estimated that only one in twenty Italian immigrants were literate, which is why so many of the letters were written by the same person.
364. This is the theory that people display characteristic and identifiable nervous tremors in their handwriting.
365. Gould was also called upon to compare the signatures of Andrew Carnegie and Cassie L. Chadwick, the con woman who had been passing herself off as Carnegie's illegitimate daughter.
366. "A Number of Marion Men Are on the Stand and Testify to the Good Character of a Couple of the Defendants," *Marion (OH) Star*, January 27, 1910.
367. Ibid.
368. Ibid.
369. Ibid.
370. Crim had earlier solved the legendary Pearl Bryan murder case.
371. Over a century later, the media reported that Sicilian police believed they had finally solved Petrosino's killing, but it was little more than hearsay.
372. "Rules of the Society of the Banana," *Marion (OH) Daily Mirror*, January 26, 1910.
373. Ibid.
374. "Justice Is Swift in Black Hand Case," *New York Times*, January 30, 1910.
375. "Hurried Off to Ft. Leavenworth," *Marion (OH) Daily Mirror*, January 31, 1910.
376. Ibid.
377. "Justice Is Swift in Black Hand Case," *New York Times*.

## Chapter 19

378. "Demanded $5,000 of President Wilson," *Barre (VT) Daily Times*, June 9, 1913.

379. "Breaking Up the Black Hand." *Manawatu (NZ) Standard*, February 1, 1910.
380. "The Society of the Banana," *(Saint Paul, MN) Appeal*, February 26, 1910.
381. "Justice Is Swift in Black Hand Case," *New York Times*.
382. "Church Black Hand Inquiry," *New York Times*, March 17, 1910.
383. Ibid.
384. "Letter of Black Hand," *Ogden (UT) Standard*, January 10, 1910.
385. "Murdered on Street," *Fort Mill (SC) Times*, June 16, 1910.
386. "Try to Blackmail Prelate," *New York Times*, October 23, 1910.
387. "Black Hand in Columbus," *(Richmond, VA) Times Dispatch*, December 18, 1911.
388. Ibid.
389. Albanese appears to have been shot to death in 1918, the victim of a justified homicide.
390. "Caruso Blackmailer Guilty," *New York Times*, May 12, 1910.
391. "Not Exactly Tickled," *Pittsburgh (PA) Post-Gazette*, March 8, 1913.
392. Ibid.
393. "Demanded $5,000 of President Wilson," *Barre (VT) Daily Times*.
394. "Wilson Receives Black Hand Note," *Licking Valley (KY) Courier*, June 12, 1913.
395. "Demanded $5,000 of President Wilson," *Barre (VT) Daily Times*.
396. Ibid.
397. "Black Hand Letter for the President," *Sacramento (CA) Union*, January 7, 1915.
398. "Black Handers Had Armory," *New York Times*, August 9, 1912.
399. Ibid.
400. "Amicon Brothers Co. to Meet Obligations and Continue in Business," *Chicago (IL) Packer*, March 3, 1928.
401. Hoover had received this assurance from Frank Costello, one of the top Mafia bosses, who, it has been suggested, provided him with tips on horse races.
402. "The Truth About J. Edgar Hoover," *Time*, December 22, 1975.

## Appendix

403. "The Society of the Banana," *(Washington, D.C.) Evening Star*, January 27, 1910.
404. "Rules of the Society of the Banana," *Marion (OH) Daily Mirror*.

# BIBLIOGRAPHY

## Books

Cawthorne, Nigel. *Mafia: The History of the Mob*. London: Arcturus, 2012.

Conley, William G. *Reports of Cases Determined by the Supreme Court of Appeals of West Virginia*. Vol. 68. Charleston, WV: Tribune Printing Company, 1911.

Franklin, Benjamin. *Observation Concerning the Increase of Mankind, Peopling of Countries, &c*. Boston: S. Kneeland, 1751.

Gambino, Richard. *Vendetta: The True Story of the Largest Lynching in U.S. History*. Montreal: Guernica Editions, 2000.

Harden, Mike. *Passage to America: The Life of Salvatore "Papa" Presutti*. Columbus, OH: Lawhead Press, 1975.

Hendley, Nate. *American Gangsters, Then and Now*. Santa Barbara, CA: Greenwood Publishing Group, 2010.

Lombardo, Robert M. *The Black Hand: Terror by Letter in Chicago*. Urbana: University of Illinois Press, 2010.

Nelli, Humbert S. *The Business of Crime: Italians and Syndicate Crime in the United States*. Chicago: University of Chicago Press, 1976.

Newton, Michael. *The Mafia at Apalachin, 1957*. Jefferson, NC: McFarland & Company, 2012.

O'Neil, John H. *Diocese of Columbus: The History of Fifty Years, 1868–1918*. Columbus, OH: self-published, 1918.

Parrington, Vernon Lewis. *The Beginnings of Critical Realism in America*. Vol. 3 New Brunswick, RI: Transaction Publishers, 2013.

Schiavo, Giovanni. *The Truth About the Mafia and Organized Crime in America.* New York: Vigo Press, 1962.

Sifakis, Carl. *The Mafia Encyclopedia.* New York: Facts on File, 2005.

Smith, James P., and Barry Edmonston, eds. *The New Americans: Economic, Demographic, and Fiscal Effects of Immigration.* Washington, D.C.: National Academy Press, 1997.

Thurber, James. *A Thurber Album.* New York: Simon and Schuster, 1952.

Wallace, Robert M. *Hegel's Philosophy of Reality, Freedom, and God.* New York: Cambridge University Press, 2005.

Whiteside, James. *Italy in the Nineteenth Century.* London: Richard Bentley, 1849.

Willis, Clint, ed. *Wise Guys: Stories of Mobsters from Jersey to Vegas.* New York: Thunder's Mouth Press, 2003.

Wilson, Woodrow. *History of the American People.* Vol. 5. New York: Harper & Brothers, 1902.

Woodwiss, Michael. *Organized Crime and American Power.* Toronto: University of Toronto Press, 2001.

## *Articles*

Baiamonte, John V., Jr. "'Who Killa de Chief' Revisited: The Hennessy Assassination and Its Aftermath, 1890–1991." *Louisiana History: The Journal of the Louisiana Historical Association* 33, no. 2 (Spring 1992).

D'Amato, Gaetano. "The 'Black Hand' Myth." *North American Review* 187, no. 629 (April 1908).

Denison, Lindsay. "The Black Hand." *Everybody's Magazine* 19, no. 3 (September 1908).

Evans, Arthur. "Crimes of Mafia Long a Terror at New Orleans." *Chicago (IL) Tribune*, September 20, 1928.

Falco, Ed. "When Italian Immigrants Were 'The Other'." CNN, accessed March 6, 2017. http://edition.cnn.com/2012/07/10/opinion/falco-italian-immigrants.

Hale, Henry. "The Menace of the Black Hand." *Wide World Magazine* 21, no. 122 (May 1908).

*Literary Digest* 38, no. 25 (June 19, 1909).

Morgan, Appleton. "What Shall We Do with the Dago?." *Popular Science Monthly* 38 (December 1890).

Oppenheimer, Francis. "The Nationality of New York Criminals." *Ohio State Journal*, March 21, 1909.

Persico, Joseph E. "Vendetta in New Orleans." *American Heritage* 24, no. 4 (June 1973).

"A Review of the World." *Current Literature* 46, no. 5 (May 1909).

White, Frank Marshall. "The Passing of the Black Hand Society." *Pearson's Magazine* 17 (March 1907).

Woods, Arthur. "In the Grip of the Black Hand." *McClure's Magazine* 33 (1909).

Wright, William Lord. "The Conflict with the 'Black Hand'." *Wide World Magazine* (1910).

# INDEX

# ABOUT THE AUTHORS

A graduate of Miami and Ohio State Universities, DAVID MEYERS has written a number of local histories and various works for the stage. Among the former are *Columbus: The Musical Crossroads* and *Ohio Jazz*, while the latter include *The Last Christmas Carol*, *The Legend of Sleepy Hollow Condominium Association* and *The Last Oz Story*. He has a background in adult and juvenile corrections.

ELISE MEYERS WALKER is a graduate of Hofstra University and served on the boards of the Columbus Historical Society and the Ted Lewis Museum in Circleville. She and her father have previously collaborated on *Central Ohio's Historic Prisons*, *Historic Columbus Crimes*, *Look to Lazarus*, *Columbus State Community College*, *Inside the Ohio Penitentiary*, *Kahiki Supper Club*, *Wicked Columbus* and *Carrying Coal to Columbus*.

*Visit us at*
www.historypress.com